FIGHT
LIKE A
GIRL

FIGHT LIKE A GRL

KYM ROCK

be scared with a plan

TATE PUBLISHING & Enterprises

Published by Tate Publishing & Enterprises, LLC
127 E. Trade Center Terrace | Mustang, Oklahoma 73064 USA
1.888.361.9473 | www.tatepublishing.com

Tate Publishing is committed to excellence in the publishing industry. The company reflects the philosophy established by the founders, based on Psalm 68:11,
"The Lord gave the word and great was the company of those who published it."

Published in the United States of America

ISBN: 978-1-61739-639-7
1. Self-Help, Abuse
2. Self-Help, Safety
10.12.16

If you are being physically abused and controlled by your significant other, they will not let you read this book.

You can remove this Fight Like a Girl cover now and throw it away somewhere your partner won't find it.

For those of you who are not in an abusive relationship, good. Keep it that way. This book will empower you to overcome trials and obstacles on your way to a full and rewarding life.

For those of you who are afraid in your daily lives, I am going to show you how to hold your head up proudly and make a new beginning for yourself.

dedication

This book is dedicated to all the women and children who have been lost as a result of a violent act. Here's to finding your way back home…

Special thanks to Alison Perry.

To my parents, John and Janet Blake, and my brother, Toby Blake, who always believed in me. I love you all. To my niece and nephew, Danielle and Jared, Aunt Kym loves you.

To my mentor and great friend, Jerry Lemon. I couldn't have done it without you!

To my best of friends: Candice Mitchem, Carole Warnecki, Debbie Knieper, Joyce Sargeant, and all the special people in my life who took a chance on something that not only did I believe in, but they did too!

To Hillary Rock. I will always be here for you!

TABLE OF CONTENTS

Introduction   *11*

part one:

Don't Go There   *17*

What Does it Mean to Fight Like A Girl?   *19*

Why You Might Be a Target   *27*

What Makes You A Target   *35*

What Group Are You In?   *43*

Telltale Signs That You Need to Stop It Now *137*

part two:

Getting Out of a Bad Situation   *143*

What Do You Do Now?   *145*

You Have Defenses   *159*

A New Philosophy   *173*

You Can Do This   *183*

End Notes   *189*

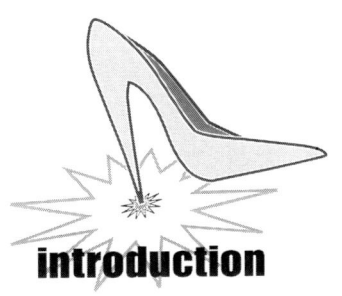

introduction

I was born and raised in the conservative farming community of Hartfield, Virginia, where, at eight years old, I challenged the redneck "bubba" thinking of the community by becoming the first female outfielder for the local little league baseball team. I always wanted to do things that were out of the norm. Especially if someone said, "Oh, you can't do that; that's for boys." I thought, Well, it looks like fun to me, and I want to do it. Why can't I have fun, too?

So my poor parents always had to endure the strange things that I wanted to do. When everyone else's little girl wanted to play with Barbies, I wanted to ride motorcycles and go-karts and the like. Although I went through the Barbie stage—complete with the Winnebago and my favorite, the

pink corvette (much more convenient than that big, old camper)—one day I discovered GI Joe.

My brother and his friends were playing with them, and I thought they were really cool because they were big, had all kinds of accessories like canteens, tools, jeeps, helmets, and they weren't fake-looking like the Barbies. The greatest part about GI Joe was that you could actually move him and bend him in different positions. When you did that with Barbie, she kind of popped and made this horrible sound like you were breaking her leg, and even then you still couldn't get her in the position you wanted!

The point is that even at a very young age, I could see that women were not in the position that men were in life.

Therefore, I always challenged anything that prevented women from doing something. I had to have a motorcycle and a go-kart. I wasn't normal. My parents can attest to that and still do! I never will forget all the times my mom would get upset because whenever it would rain, my brother and I would head out the door. You see, go-karts do 360s best in the rain. By the time we were through making donuts in the yard, you could have sworn there was a Krispy Kreme stand out there.

But even though my parents would have rather seen me play with dolls and the like, they still tried very hard to be supportive of whatever I wanted to do. Support is the key word. I continued to excel in sports by becoming one of the first females on the high school soccer team. Our team did quite well, and, as a matter of fact, we won the state championship several times. I remember coming into the house with mud up one side and down the other, and my mom saying, "Stop. Stop in your tracks; take that mess off in the garage." Then she would ask, "How did you do? Did you win?" I don't think she liked watching the games too much because soccer is rather rough, but she was always supportive of me in whatever I did. Moms and dads, you should learn from them. Your kids may need your emotional support just as much later in life as they did when they were little.

I do believe that everything happens for a reason, and we are put in tough situations to see what we will do with the experiences when they're over. Shortly after high school, I found myself in a mentally and

physically abusive relationship. My parents warned me. I should have listened to them.

I suffered through verbal abuse, being choked, having dinners thrown in the floor, my arm slammed in the door, trips to the emergency room, being chased through the house with a snake, of which I was terrified, and a lot more. However, you have to ask, "What am I going to do about it?" Are you going to sulk and say, "Oh, poor me. Why is this happening? I don't understand." Of course, you'll say that. It's what I said too. Ultimately, though, you have to make a plan and take action to set yourself free.

After I had decided that I had had enough, I started driving about an hour and fifteen minutes from my home to take karate classes. Eventually, through the physical and mental discipline that it teaches, I rediscovered the self-esteem that I had somehow lost. Shortly after realizing how bad my situation really was, with the help of my karate instructor, I started planning how I could get out of it. The planning paid off, and since then I haven't looked back. I realized that I have the power within myself to effect positive change and that I have a passion for helping others. I knew then that I had to pass on what I had learned through my difficult experiences to those who truly need it.

I relocated to North Carolina's Outer Banks, where I was determined to help those in similar predicaments take back control of their lives. I began to learn new skills in rape and abduction prevention, police defense tactics, weapons, and mental concentration. Although I had competed for years in the martial arts and had a great winning career in local and state competitions, I felt that those successes weren't enough. I wanted more. There was a hunger I could not satisfy. Even after becoming the National Karate Champion in Weapons and Kata and World Weapons and Kata Champion seven times—with many other inductions into the United State Martial Arts Hall of Fame and the World Karate Union Hall of Fame—there was still an empty void.

Therefore, in 1995 I founded the Outer Banks Karate Studio in Nags Head, North Carolina, and have led sixty-three students to their black belt certification. I found that my passion lies in making a difference in people's lives and in helping them create positive changes within themselves. After almost twenty years in the industry, I have finally gained the self-respect and satisfaction that I had been seeking for a long time.

My passion is you—helping you rebuild your self-esteem and empowering you to feel better about yourself. If you are in an abusive relationship, I want to help you pick yourself up and get out of your current situation or a potentially dangerous one. I want us all to prevent future oppressive situations for everyone. Helping women through the knowledge that I have acquired is the best paycheck I could ever receive.

I have developed and adapted simple ways for you to keep yourself and your family safe. You do not have to be a karate expert to save yourself or protect your children. All you have to do is turn the page and be willing to take action. This book can and will help every woman who reads it. Someone told me once, "One person can make a difference. One person with an army behind them can change the world." Won't you become a member of this army? Learn how to help yourself so you can help others.

Part One:

DON'T GO THERE

what does it mean
to fight like a girl?

Webster's New World Dictionary says that fight means "to take part in a struggle, contest, etc. especially against a foe or for a cause." Here is what it means to us: "We are going to stand up for what's right. We are going to battle this!" Whatever "this" may be. Stand up, for God's sake! Whatever it is in your life that is getting in your way, that is keeping you from living a full and rewarding life, overcome it. If you can't climb over it, go around it or through it, then hitch a ride with someone who has the vehicle to help you climb over your obstacle—and that doesn't necessarily mean an automobile.

There is a resource or person somewhere in your life that can help you. You have to think smarter so you can turn your instinctive responses into effective self-defense. Remember, self-defense doesn't necessarily have to mean physical self-defense. From this day forward, the phrase "fight like a girl" does not represent weakness; it stands for empowerment. It means being smarter and more aware in your life. The next time someone says, "Hey, you fight like a girl!" your response is going to be, "You bet I do!"

> Self: Person, identity; your identity
> Defense: Protection, security

> Fight Like a Girl is a mind-set, a sense of empowerment that can be applied daily to everyday decisions. It is to protect yourself, defend your identity, and secure your self-worth.

> Be aware!
> Walk with intent!
> Do your job with purpose!
> Empower your mind in your daily routine!

"How?" you may ask. Here are some examples of how to Fight Like A Girl. If you go to work every night at the same time and clock in around 11:30

p.m., there may be a parking space over in the corner that is rather dark and secluded. You may already be running late, but something in your brain tells you to not park there. You listen! You're thinking. It's just like the spider and the cobweb. As long as you stay away from it, you don't get caught in the web, so just leave that spider alone.

A spider web is just like something that's out of place, hanging around where it shouldn't be, ready to snatch you up when you least expect it. Remember how quickly you can be covered in that sticky web before you ever even saw it? Pay attention! Be aware! Look around you. Listen. If you see that web of something out of place, keep your distance. Compare these two photos. Can you see why I compare a spider to something that is out of place?

You are more likely to be a target if you are sheepish, timid, or walk like you have your tail between your legs. Guess what? You are not an animal! It's time you stop being treated like one. Get it? The decisions you make every moment can determine the outcome at the end of your day. Do you agree? Well, if so, then make smart choices as you go through the day. For example, always make sure you have a full tank of gas in your car. I know. It's raining, and it's cold. "I think I can make it home," you think or, "It's only a few more miles to the $2.23 cents per gallon gas station! I can make it! I can make it!" you say.

Suppose you get home and find out there are intruders in your house, and you try to leave, but your car won't start? Suppose you have an emergency in the middle of the night? There may not be anywhere to get gas that late. Your adrenaline gets up, and you totally forget that you didn't feel like getting gas on the way home. Guess what? You're in trouble! Daily decisions! Daily decisions! Stop living in the white zone. It's that simple. These little daily decisions that we make really can and do affect our future. So the best decision is to always listen to your gut, trust your instincts, and don't be lazy. Just stop and get some gas, girl.

The Fight Like a Girl ethic provides noncon-frontational responses that not only can be applied to your personal safety but also to your work skills by allowing you to diffuse situations through body language. In these photos, can you tell who is using body language to their benefit?

This is the basis for Fight Like a Girl. Although this book is geared for women and children, the Fight Like a Girl ethic can be used and applied by everyone: men, women, preteens, teens, college students, and children.

why you might be a target

Because you are a woman…

Because someone feels misunderstood…

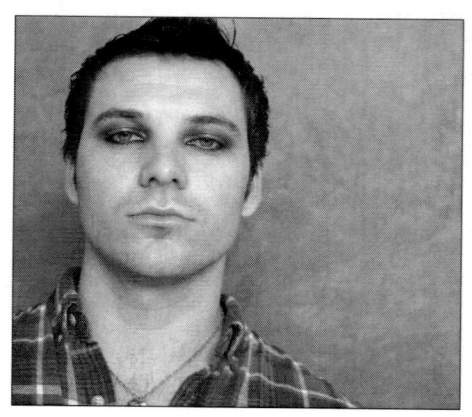

Simply because of the color of your skin...

Because someone believes they control you...

Because you're old...

Because you're dating someone else...

Because you appear to be rich...

Because you thought you were talking to someone your own age...

Because you came to work…

Don't be a victim. Start by appearing to be confident.

what makes you a target?

As a woman, that's pretty obvious, isn't it? Let me think. Through the ages, we have been billed as the weaker sex. The truth is, as far as strength, men are indeed physically stronger than us. They may be stronger, but that doesn't make them smarter. That's where we come in, ladies.

There is no way I can fling an average-sized man on the ground using just my strength. Even though I consider myself to be pretty strong, I cannot rely on that to get me out of a dangerous situation. This is why we are targets. We are, indeed, the physically weaker sex. There's that word again. Sex. There lies the issue. Two things in this world that can create a lot of problems: money and sex. This is what makes you and your children a target—and ladies, we are all potential targets.

The Facts:

- 9 out of every 10 rape victims are female.

- 1 in 5 women and 1 in 33 men have experienced an attempted or completed rape.[2]

- 1 in 4 women will experience domestic violence in their lifetimes.[3]

- Females who are 20 to 24 years of age are at the greatest risk for sexual assault, rape, or murder.[4]

- One-third of female homicide victims who are reported in police records are killed by an intimate partner.[5]

- 7.8 million women have been raped by an intimate partner at some point in their lives.[6]

- The cost of intimate partner violence exceeds $5.8 billion each year, $4.1 billion of which is direct medical and mental health services.[7]

- Witnessing violence between one's parents or care-takers is the strongest risk factor of transmitting violent behavior from one generation to the next.[8]

- 77 million women/girls are physically assaulted every year in the United States.[9]

- While about 80 percent of all victims are white, minorities are somewhat more likely to be attacked.[10]

- 67 percent of rape incidents occur at nighttime between 6 p.m. and 6 a.m.[11]

- 80 percent of the victims of rape and sexual assault in the workplace are women.[12]

Here's the math: According to the U.S. Department of Justice's National Crime Victimization Survey—the country's largest and most reliable crime study—there were 248,300 sexual assaults in 2007 (the most recent data available). There are 525,600 minutes in a non-leap year. That makes 31,536,000 seconds/year. So, 31,536,000 divided by 248,300 comes out to one sexual assault every 127 seconds, or about one every two minutes.[13]

As you can see, just being a woman or a child in our country means that you are a target. It shouldn't be this way.

It's time to fight back, ladies; it's time to be smarter. Take a look at the facts above. Statistics don't lie. It

is up to us to start rallying with our school systems, our collegiate systems, our churches, and our communities to instill these self-protective measures for our children and ourselves. We as women need to stand up, be empowered, and find the funding that is needed to educate our children and ourselves, or we will remain targets. It doesn't have to be this way. You can take simple steps in your everyday decision-making that mean the difference between victimization and freedom.

Here is just one example of how we can all become a victim just from a lack of awareness:

scary incident for everyone

This came from an Internet circulation:

Know what money you are carrying. This was the first I have heard of a scheme like this…I wanted to pass it along. Be safe! This is something very serious. Criminals are coming up with craftier, less threatening methods of attack, so we have to be extra cautious. This incident occurred while a serial killer was active in the Louisiana area. Read on.

It was approximately 5:15 a.m. in Opelousas, Louisiana; I had stayed with a friend there and was on my way to work. I stopped at the Exxon/Blimpie Pie station to get gas. I got ten-dollars worth of gas and a Diet Coke. I took into the store two five-dollar bills and one one-dollar bill (just enough to get my stuff). As I pulled away from the store, a man approached my truck from the back of the store, an unlit area. He was an "approachable-looking" man (clean cut, clean shaven, well dressed). He walked up to my window and knocked. Since I'm very paranoid and always looking for the rapist or killer, I didn't open the window. I just asked what he wanted. He raised a five-dollar bill to my window and said, "You dropped this." Since I knew I had gone into the store with a certain amount of money, I knew I didn't drop it. When I told him it wasn't mine, he began hitting the window and door, screaming at me to open my door and insisting that I had dropped the money. At that point, I just drove away as fast as I could.

After talking to the Internal Affairs Department and describing the man I saw and the way he escalated from calm and polite to angry and volatile, it was determined that I could have possibly encountered the serial killer myself. Up to this point, it had been unclear as to how he had gained access to his victims, since there has been no evidence of forced entry into victims' homes, cars, etc. The fact that he has been attacking in the daytime, when women are less likely to have their guard up, means he is pretty bold. So think about it; what gesture is nicer than returning money to someone who dropped it?

How many times would you have opened your window (or door) to get your money and say thank you…because if the person is kind enough to return something to you, then he can't really be a threat, can he? Please be cautious! This might not have been the serial killer, but anyone who gets that angry over someone not accepting money from them can't have honorable intentions. The most important thing to note is that his reaction was not what I expected! A total surprise. But what might have happened if I had opened my door? I shudder to think. Ladies, really do tell everyone you know about this. Even if this man wasn't a serial killer, he looked nice, he seemed polite, he was apparently doing an act of kindness, but he was not a nice person!

what group are you in?

Now that I have explained to you why you are a target, let's take some steps to keep you from being one. First, let's determine what category you are in. There are thirteen we are going to address: babies, toddlers, schoolchildren (five- to seven-year-olds), young girls and boys (eight- to ten-year-olds), the tweens (eleven- and twelve-year-olds), teens, college students, single women, single moms, female executives, the totally oblivious, current stalking victims, and domestic violence victims.

babies

First of all, a baby can't protect itself. It's up to you. If you're pregnant, guess what? You're a target. Please, don't be insulted. Let's face it. I do not want to upset you, but when you are eight to nine months pregnant, you're kind of hard to miss. There are people watching you, thinking about it... Really thinking, "Why can she can have a baby and I can't?" or "Wow, I could get a lot of money for that baby. That could really help me get the drugs I need", or "The John Doe's said they would pay me $100,000 to find them a baby. I could get away with it. She can't move that fast. I could just take the baby right out of her belly." That's pretty sick, isn't it? I don't mean to be so graphic, but it is so true. These horrible things do happen—regularly.

There are men and women who will do anything to have a child or get a child. Your baby is worth a lot of money on the black market. According to chacha.com, the baby you're about to have is worth between $4,000 and $35,000 to someone else. I can't even imagine the thought of what it would be like to lose a child under any circumstances, and I don't want you to lose yours. I especially don't want your baby to end up with someone who has no morals, someone who wants a baby so badly that they will use their money and hire criminal kidnappers to take your child—or just attack you and snatch your baby themselves.

So, as a pregnant woman, what can you do to protect yourself and your unborn baby from these predators? Well, as you progress in your pregnancy, be very wary of people whom you really do not know coming up to you and saying, "Congratulations! When are you due? My cousin just had a beautiful baby boy at the hospital just down the road. Do you know the one?" This stranger is fishing to find out if you're local. They may even wait and follow you to see where you live. Crazy? Yes. Does it happen? Yes. So, be cautious with a conversation like this, and when someone asks you when you are due, don't give them a date or any information other than, "My husband and I are very excited. He's a police officer, and we didn't think we could afford a baby right now, but we decided to go for it!" Smile and move on with your day.

As you move along further in your pregnancy, people will offer to help you carry bags, lift things, etc. There are just plain, good people in this world, and not everyone has ill intent, but keep your guard up. Pay attention to the interaction and move away from those who seem to ask out-of-place questions or appear too frequently.

As you are further along in your pregnancy, have someone accompany you on your errands. You shouldn't be lifting heavy things or overdoing it at this point in your pregnancy, anyway. Don't answer the door when you're home alone, especially if it is a woman you don't know. In the past, women have knocked on the door of a pregnant (or recently pregnant) woman's home to say that their car was broken down and, after being let in to use the phone,

attacked the woman and stole her newborn baby. At this point in your life, let them go to someone else's house to use the phone. Seriously, it's okay.

Here are some safety tips you can follow to keep your child safe from a stranger abduction or from a family abduction.

1. Are you estranged from the baby's father and his parents? If so, you may need to be particularly diligent in your abduction awareness.

2. Always keep a baby monitor next to your child's crib.

3. Never have your baby's crib next to a window.

4. A security system is mandatory! No exceptions. You need one not just for intruders but also in case of fire or emergency. Get one.

5. If daycare will be required for your new baby, be specific as to who can pick up your child; have it in writing.

6. If grandparents will be helping take care of your new baby, make sure they also follow your safety rules.

7. When shopping, never put your child in the car first. I have heard of so many cars being stolen with the child in the back. There's a simple way to prevent this common trick. Unlock the car door, back the shopping cart up to the car so your baby is next to you and the long part of the cart is putting distance between you and anyone who would approach. Throw your bags in, throw your purse in, still have keys in your hand, place your child in the car seat, shut the door and leave the shopping cart where it is. Look around, hop in the driver's seat, lock the doors, start the car, and leave. (When you have a young child, it's okay to leave the cart safely pushed off to the side. The stores pay people to bring them back inside. Never leave your child in the car alone to return a cart.)

8. Never leave kids alone in a car or a stroller, not even for a minute.

9. Have ID-like photos taken of your children every six months, and have them fingerprinted. Keep your kids' dental and medical records up to date. If they are ever missing, these will help expedite the search efforts.

toddlers

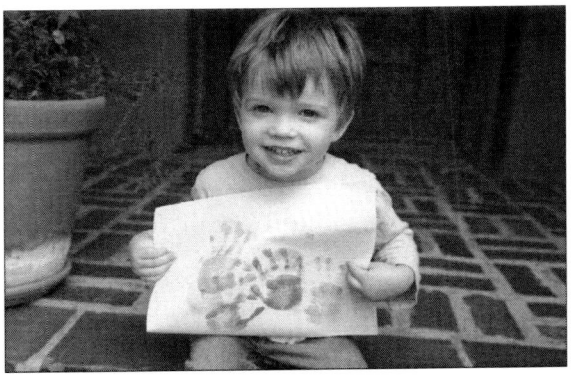

The number of children reported missing in the U.S. is about 800,000 every year, and according to Kids-health, about 2,100 kids are reported missing daily. Fifty-eight thousand children were abducted in 2002 by non-family perpetrators, according to the national incidence studies of missing, abducted, runaway, and thrown-away children. Statistically, going with the current USA population clock, on March 25, 2010, at almost 309 million, toddlers comprise 33 percent of the population, of which 4 percent will be victims of abduction, sexual molestation, abuse, or murder.[1] That's approximately 42,000 toddlers per year...in the United States alone. Does this enormous number surprise you?

This figure sounds bad, but as you will see, the figures grow tremendously worse as your children get older. At this age, they are more protected by you, and that is why the percentages are lower. Independence is not quite part of their daily routine, yet.

The number one way a child is abducted is by a vehicle. Toddlers are a scary category. There is only so much they can do, but if it makes you feel any better, this is actually the age group with the lowest percentage of abductions. Although it seems more prevalent in the news, the main reason is, these abductions get more international coverage. It really tugs at our heartstrings to know that someone has taken a little boy or girl. Let's reduce this percentage even further. The first thing you can do is talk, talk, and talk some more about these things to your small children. Repetition is key, but sadly, studies show that even kids who have been told time and time again about stranger danger, when tested, were tempted to stray away from their parent with someone they did not know.

Using the old, "Can you help me find my puppy or kitty?" trick, predators break down the few defenses young children may have. Even worse, they may have a cute little pet in their hands to draw the children to them. This is the worst! It is so hard for anyone to resist a cute, little animal. The predator will tell the child something like, "I have another puppy in the car, and I will give it to you. Come on… We can go get it, and then you can surprise your mom."

Use the old arm's-length rule and keep your kids within arm's length and in your line of sight when you're in public with them. Adhere to this especially when you are in big department stores, where it is so easy to lose sight of your child. It only takes seconds for your life to be changed forever, leaving you and your family with an emptiness that will never be filled. Once a toddler is gone, the likelihood you will get them back in one piece is very slim. Prevention is the key. Role-playing works much better than just talking to your kids. To be safe, you need to do both. Here are some role-playing skills and even some self-defense tips that your little tike can use to get away from a stranger.

Self-defense tips for little tikes:

- Temper tantrums! You may not have to show them how to throw one, but this is exactly what they should do if someone coerces them into a car and they find themselves in trouble. Teach them how to drop and kick, even if you only have them by one hand. Have them practice kicking your shins and screaming (preferably after you've talked about stranger danger and not in the grocery store).

- Pick them up from behind and have them throw their head backwards forcefully, hitting you with the back of their head while kicking you as hard as they can with their heels and squirming. Perhaps you should use a pillow so you don't get too beat up! This can be effective in causing someone to put them down so they can run away. No one wants a toddler that's going to be that much trouble all the time.

- Teach your toddler to bite…when appropriate. This is what you do: Go to the grocery store and buy a few tangelos. The skin of the tangelo simulates human skin, so make them bite the tangelo with a small, strong bite using just their front teeth and rip the bite to the side. They have to do this until there is a tear on the surface of the tangelo; then put them down and let them go. They will remember this because it worked and the reward was that they were set free. Also, the bitter taste from the tangelo peel is something they will not forget.

- Role play: Grab a stuffed animal that's really cute and say to your child, "If an adult comes up to you in a car, near our yard (most abductions occur within a quarter mile from the victim's house), or at the store with a little puppy or kitten and asks you to come closer, turn around and run the other way." Explain to them what a trick is and how it can be a mean trick. Let them know that if a stranger asks them to help look for a missing pet or earring or friend or offers them candy, that they should run the other way to a trusted adult and tell them immediately what happened.

- The number one way kids are abducted is from the street, lured into vehicles. Teach your child that an adult doesn't need to ask them for anything—directions or any help—especially when they are near a vehicle or street.

- Some people may not like them, but I'd say to use one of the popular child tethers. I see nothing wrong with having your toddler connected to you. They are still free to walk, but if they get too far away, you can reel them back in, and no one can take them without you knowing and being close enough to do something about it.

girls and boys: five to seven years old

By now, your kids are in pre-school or elementary school. The good news is, child abductions from a schoolyard are rare. Here's the problem, though: now they have more independence and are surrounded by older kids and adults. Some may even walk home from school by themselves. However, at this age, I believe this is just unacceptable. I do not care how close your house may or may not be to the school. This is how your kids get taken, and this is how they get abducted just steps from your own yard.

Listen to this: They are simply walked away. Pedophiles do not have a certain look. They look like the guy next door or the kid who rakes your yard. That's right. Many children that are molested are molested by other kids under the age of seventeen. It's up to you, as a parent, to be as close to your kids as possible at this age. Arm's-length rule once again. For goodness's sake, they are only five to seven years old!

They should not be riding their bikes up and down the neighborhood without a trusted adult supervis-

ing, no matter how safe you think it is. Guess what? It's not safe! Either you, as the parent, be outside where you can keep them in view, or they can go riding with an older brother or sister. Safety in numbers always. Here are a few things you can do to help your kids and others in this age group:

1. Confidence rules. They need to walk like they are going to be a pain in the butt if you even think about touching them.

2. Enroll them in karate classes—no ifs, ands, or buts—but make sure it is a reputable school with good morals, quality instructors, and a successful kids' program that teaches life and safety skills.

3. Get them a dog. Dogs are protective of the kids they grow up with, and they will know when danger is around. Kidnappers are less likely to take a child who has a big buddy or medium-sized buddy on a leash with them. Even the friendliest, most laid-back dog will take a stand when a stranger threatens their kid.

4. When answering the phone, a child should never say, "Mommy's not here," or "Daddy's not here." Instead, teach them to say that you are in the shower or on the computer, or "Daddy's working on a proj-

ect. Do you want me to go get him?" Train your kids. Test your kids. Please!

5. Teach your child to never answer the door when they are home alone.

6. Don't hide the key to your house outside if your child comes home alone after school. A predator will easily watch and learn where you keep the key to the house. Make sure your child has their own key and teach them to look around before approaching the door and letting themselves in. Once they are inside, they should lock the door behind them.

7. Don't embroider your child's name on everything. If you do, then a stranger can call him or her by his or her first name, which lets down their defenses and gives the kidnapper an opportunity to create trust. Use a laundry pen and write their name on the inside of their backpack if necessary.

8. Have an emergency password between you and your child and explain the importance of the emergency password. A password is only used once. For example: You call home at three fifteen to make sure your child is home safely; their emergency password is "popcorn." You say, "Hi, honey. I'm just checking on you to make sure you're home okay?" Your child says, "Well, I'm just having some popcorn." You

know your child hates popcorn and would never eat it; that is why you chose the emergency word. Your reply is, "Did you just use our emergency popcorn password?" Your child repeats, "Yes ma'am, I'm just having popcorn." You say, "Okay, I'll see you soon," and hang up and dial 911. More than likely, someone is in the house. It wouldn't help the situation for the child to create a sense of urgency or anger the stranger in the house. Passwords can be used in different situations, and it's up to you to decide who gets to know the child's emergency password. It's important that someone you trust knows the password for your child in case there is an emergency and they can't reach you.

general internet use for five- to seven-year-olds

A few things you may not have considered about letting your young child use the computer…

1. Kindergarten through first-grade students access the Internet using various devices for a variety of purposes, including playing online games and communicating with other people. Online gaming is increasingly popular among younger students.

2. Forty-eight percent of kindergarten- to first-grade-level students interact with people on websites. Fifty percent indicate that their parents watch them when they use a computer, leaving the other half of those youngsters more prone to being exposed to predator behaviors or other threats posed by online strangers or even persons they know or regard as friends.

3. Forty-eight percent of kindergarten to first-grade students reported viewing online content that made them feel uncomfortable. Seventy-two percent reported the experience to a grown-up, meaning that one in four children did not say anything to an adult.[2]

It's important to be with your kids when they are on the Internet at this age, or better yet, download or install games they may want to play. Then, disconnect the computer from the Internet while they're using it for games or typing. You can get parental and Internet controls that can be effective at this age, because while most kids are more tech savvy than their parents, you might be able to stay one step ahead of your five-year-old!

young girls and boys: eight- to ten-year-olds

Unfortunately, the older your children get, the more they are at risk for several reasons. For one, with age comes more freedom, and with more freedom, more risk. The percentages of incidents have once again gone up. Talk to your kids about these risk issues a lot at this age. They understand and remember more, so the more you nag them about these safety issues, the better.

Non-Family abductions:

- More than 65 percent of the children abducted by non-family members are girls, according to the Baltimore Crime Examiner, Arlene Karridis.

- 46 percent of children are sexually abused.

- 31 percent of the children are physically abused.

- 32 percent of abductions take place in a street by a car, and 25 percent take place in a park or a wooded area.

- The top three places an abductor imprisons the child are a car, the abductor's home, and the abductor's building.

- Most abductions occur within a quarter of a mile of the child's home.

- 75 percent of the abductors are male.

- 67 percent of them are below 29 years of age.

Stereotypical kidnappings:

- 40 percent of children in "stereotypical" kidnappings are killed.

- 4 percent of children are never found.

- 79 percent of kidnappings are carried out by strangers and 21 percent by acquaintances.

- Nearly 75 percent of the parents in the U.S. fear that their children might become victims of abduction.[3]

out and about

As parents, we may feel that certain places near our home, in our neighborhood, or nearby parks are safe for our kids. However, the fact is that with their newfound freedom to be out and about without your supervision, the probability of abduction has increased. You have to look differently at familiar places when evaluating their safety for your child to be there with their friends and without your presence. One thing is a given: There is safety in numbers. Make it your policy!

Your mom was right on this one. Period! There is safety in numbers. Have your child travel with a group of friends whenever they walk around town or go to a park. Make certain they understand that they are never, ever to leave without everyone. As a parent, you also need to have time restrictions! We all know that we cannot lock our children up in the house until they are eighteen. They can't always be in a group, and they will be out on their own sometimes.

So, have a time limit on how long it should take them to get from place to place. For a friend's house in the neighborhood, actually time it yourself. Go with them the first time—at their pace, not yours. Then in the future, that is how much time you should allow for them to get there. If there is not a phone call from your child letting you know they arrived right on the button, then you are to call the neighbor's house and check on them. If they forgot to call, then guess what? Get in the car, bike, or walk, and go get them. No matter how mad they may be about having to come right home, they will learn how important safety and responsibility are.

When I practiced this with my daughter, she was very angry when I went to go pick her up because she did not call. However, after a couple of times, not only did it become a habit with her, but other families in the neighborhood would practice this rule as well. Which, in turn, got the parents involved, and they would remind her, "Don't forget to call home!" Adults should also practice this habit of knowing how long it takes to travel and calling when they arrive safely. To this day, my mom calls to make sure

I have gotten home all right. She knows how long it takes for me to get home, and she always calls when it's time. This is not rocket science. It is just a little extra effort that can save a life—the life of your child. Practice this habit with friends of your kids to help keep them safe as well. Pass it on. You are in the Fight Like A Girl Army now! Let's train more people to help keep our kids safe!

communications

I'm sure they've been nagging, and it may seem like a silly request, but your child really should have a cell phone! Kids are carrying their own cell phones at younger and younger ages, but it is necessary to stay connected with them, especially today. If you are going to give your child the freedom to go to the park or places after school or out and about town with friends, then these preventive measures are necessary. Make sure there is good cellular signal in your calling area and with the company to which you subscribe. This way you know that you can have access to your children at all times.

The first time your child doesn't answer or call you right back immediately, then you will have to ground them and keep them at home. I only had to do this a couple of times, and after that, our daughter would make sure that she was close to her cell phone whenever she wasn't with us and would answer or call back immediately.

Now, you may say, "Well, I'm a single parent, and I can't afford a cell phone." Still, you need to make a way. If you are on a budget, you can purchase a pay-as-you-go-by-the-minute card. Cut back on something. Choose some things that may not be so great for you anyway and eliminate them from your life and your budget. Do what you have to do to keep your kids safe.

a kid's best friend

Another good point, as my dad once said, "I know why all these kids are being abducted. When is the last time you saw a kid with a big dog with them? In my day, no one had better have touched me! My dog, Butch, would've torn 'em up!" You know, he is right. With our busy lifestyles and so many community restrictions these days, it is hard for a family to have a kid and a big dog. However, animals sense danger, and they care about that little kid they grew up with.

If it's an option for you, a sizable dog can be a great deterrent and protector of you and your children.

If you can't have a dog at your home or apartment or building complex, then teach your child how to properly carry and use pepper spray. If you are going to give them the freedom to travel about by themselves, then you must take preventive steps to protect them. Does this sound extreme? Of course it does, but I would rather my child come home safely than not ever see them again because I was too cool to seem protective.

internet access

Today, the Internet plays a huge role in crimes against children between the ages of six and twelve. According to Crimes Against Children Research Center, 67 percent of offenders who committed Internet sex crimes against minors, possessed child pornography. The vast majority of offenders were non-Hispanic, white males older than twenty-five who were acting alone. Eighty percent had images explicitly showing sexual penetration of minors on their computer. Of these possessors, 83 percent had images of children between the ages of six and twelve. Pretty sick, isn't it?

Guess what? You need to monitor your child's computer. Let's face it; they are pre-teens, they are curious, and they really do not know who they are talking to in chat rooms. They may think it is someone their age, and it is not. Or even worse, they may know they are talking to an adult, and they think it's cool that they are interested in them. The next thing you know, bam! The sick predator has lured your child to meet them at another location and it's too late to protect them.

The key to stopping the violence is education. Educate yourself and your child. Go to these sites: U.S. Department of Justice, Cyber Angels Internet Safety Organization, National Coalition for the Protection of Children & Families, National Center for Missing and Exploited Children, and, my favorite Internet safety overview for parents, Enough is Enough. The Internet is a key player in crimes against our youth, and I will be covering more things you can do as a parent to monitor what your child is doing on the computer.

Beyond the computer is human trafficking – where your child could end up if they meet a "friend"

from the Internet unsupervised. Human trafficking is a $19 billion industry. Studies indicate that child prostitutes serve between two and thirty clients per week, leading to a shocking estimated 100 to 1,500 clients per year, per child. Younger children, many below the age of ten, have been increasingly drawn into serving tourists.[4]

It makes me sick just to think about these facts—and they are reality. That's why I am trying to do something about it. One person can make a difference. Two people can make a major change. You're reading this book, aren't you? Knowledge is power. Even just you and I together can make enough changes to save the lives of these kids.

tweens

You have a tween on your hands! Bet you already picked up on the change, huh? Now the odds of an attack against your child just went up even higher—22 percent! That's right. Kids between the ages of twelve and fourteen make up 22 percent of abductions and assaults. Why? Prepubescent kids are more at risk because they are curious about their bodies and the changes that are occurring within them. Perpetrators know this too, and use it to their advantage.

Forty percent of these kids who are abducted are victims of a stereotypical kidnapping by a stranger involving elements of a heinous crime, such as being abducted overnight, taken long distances, held for ransom, or killed. Of those in this group, 40 percent were killed and 4 percent were never recovered. There was no closure for their family and friends, just emptiness and loss from a tragedy.

Eighty-one percent of all non-family abducted children are age twelve or older[5] Are you worried yet? You should be. You need to take action! What can you do?

Girls are the predominant victims. This is your child, your daughter, at risk. Wouldn't it be nice if your daughter actually learned a handful of things that could save her? Teach her to fight back with everything she has. Scream! Kick! Punch! Bite! Whatever she has to do to get away. Teach your children the importance of never being taken to a second location—ever. The proof is in the pudding. Just remember MicKenzie Smith, who was grabbed and put in a man's truck in 2005 in Utah.

Her parents had talked to her frequently about fighting back if anything like this ever happened to her. She fought back so much and made such a fuss that the would-be abductor put her out of the truck! That's what we need to happen more often!

Latchkey kids are at a higher risk than most. Often, kids are home alone after school as a result of divorce or single parenting. This is an immediate attraction to a pedophile. In most cases, a child predator will befriend the adult first, becoming a familiar face and breaking down the barriers that would alert your child to danger. Please do not lay a guilt trip on yourself because you cannot afford after-school childcare. Instead of doing that, let's do this: teach your child proper defenses and procedures, such as the proper way to answer the phone when you aren't home.

Just as for your younger kids, when you call to check on your older kid after school, your child should have a password to alert you to an emergency if they are not free to speak. A password is for emergencies only, is only used once, and works like this: Choose something your child would never eat. Let's use bananas, for an example. You call to check on them and say, "Hi, honey. Mommy is just checking to see that you are in the house okay." Your child says, "Yes, ma'am, I am just sitting here, watching TV and eating a banana." The password was just used by your child! Maybe someone is in the house with them that should not be there. Now you would say, "Honey, did you say banana? You just used the password." Your child says, "Yes, I already told you that I had a banana." You say, "Okay, I am calling the police." Hang up and dial 911 immediately.

That is one way you can help your child be safe in your absence. If your child is home alone and answers the phone, teach them to never ever say they are alone. Tell them to say that, "Dad is in the garage" or "He's working on a project."

Communication is the key to saving our children and making an impact on these enormous statistics. You have to talk to your kids about situations that may come up and prepare them to act to save themselves. On your part, make sure you know where your child is and where they are going all the time. Call and check to make sure they got there safely and are comfortable with the people around them. Use all the traveling in groups and timed trips rules we discussed previously. Don't think that because you discussed these things with your kids when they were eight year old that they're going to keep them in the forefront of their minds during a tween temptation. You have to enforce that the same rules apply now and always even though they're older.

internet for tweens and teens

The Internet plays a big role in allowing access to young adults by perpetrators. Computers are necessary. Just about every home has a computer or access to one. Where there is access to the Internet, there are predators waiting to chat with your child online. The curiosity that young adults naturally have about their bodies and about sex is the loaded gun. According to the non-profit Internet crime-fighting site Enough is Enough, the predominant sex crime scenario doesn't involve violence or stranger molesters posing online as children; only 5 percent of offenders concealed the fact they were adults from their victims.

Almost 80 percent of offenders are explicit about their intentions with youth. In 73 percent of crimes, youth go to meet the predator on multiple occasions for multiple sexual encounters. Teens are willing to meet with strangers; 16 percent of teens considered meeting someone they'd only talked to online. Four percent of all youth Internet users received aggressive sexual solicitations, which threatened to spill over into "real life." These solicitors asked to meet the youth in person, called them on the telephone, or sent offline mail, money, or gifts. Also, 4 percent of youth Internet users had distressing sexual solicitations that left them feeling upset or extremely afraid. It is up to you, the adult, to educate your children about chatting with people they don't know online and the fact that there are adults who may be pretending to be kids but are really adults looking for a way to eventually meet them in person.

Your Internet service provider can provide filters and blocks that will flag certain words that are used on your child's computer. They will be more than happy to educate you about these features. You can also trace every page that your child has viewed and follow up with them about any inappropriate contact or materials they may have discovered. Limit your child's time on the computer. I know we are all guilty of using the computer for a babysitter occasionally, but it is not healthy for a child to be in front of a computer for more than two hours a day. Unless they are working on a report for school or doing research, you should limit their undirected exploring time to something appropriate.

It is very important that you monitor the websites your child is visiting. According to Harris Interactive-McAfee, a quarter of teens would be

shocked, one in five would feel hurt, and 34 percent would feel offended if they found out their mother was keeping track of what they did online without their knowledge or permission.

Talk to your kids about what is appropriate and what is not and why. Let them know that you intend to protect them and make sure they're making smart decisions but that you expect them to think safety and behave accordingly while online.

Then, you can purchase software to monitor where your child is going online. It would be a good idea to install this on their computer when they are not at home. After all, your kids are smart, and here is a list below of just some of the ways they can keep you, the parent, in the dark:

- 32 percent of teens clear the browser history to hide what they do online from their parents.

- 16 percent have created private e-mail addresses or social networking profiles to hide what they do online from their parents.

- 63 percent of teens said they know how to hide what they do online from their parents.

- 43 percent have closed or minimized the browser at the sound of a parental step.

- 11 percent have unlocked or disabled parental and filtering controls.

- 52 percent of teens have given out personal information online to someone they don't know offline, including 24 percent of whom gave personal photos and/or physical descriptions of themselves.

- Double the number of teen girls have shared photos or physical descriptions of themselves online as boys (34 percent girls versus 15 percent boys).

- 20 percent of teens have engaged in cyberbullying behaviors, including posting mean or hurtful information or embarrassing pictures, spreading rumors, publicizing private communications, sending anonymous e-mails, or cyberpranking someone.[6]

In another study, 42 percent of Internet users, aged ten to seventeen, surveyed said they had seen online pornography in a recent twelve-month span. Of those, 66 percent said they did not want to view the images and had not sought them out. The survey has a margin of error of plus or minus 2.5 percentage points. The results came from a telephone survey of 1,500 Internet users, aged ten to seventeen, conducted in 2005, with their parents' consent. In the survey, most kids who reported unwanted exposure were aged thirteen to seventeen. Still, sizable numbers of ten- and eleven-year-olds also had unwanted exposure—17 percent of boys and 16 percent of girls that age.[7]

According to our latest survey, 93 percent of all Americans between twelve and seventeen years old use the Internet. In 2004, 87 percent were Internet users, and in 2000, 73 percent of teens went online.[8]

It is your job to keep your children safe using all the knowledge and resources you can. American teens are more wired now than ever before and just as curious about their bodies and sex as you were. Some things haven't changed, but your kids' access to people and information far surpasses what you could get your hands on at that age!

what can you do to make a difference?

To get them engaged in their real life and leave them less time for idle Internet wandering, get them involved in karate or some kind of martial arts at an early age, and keep them involved until they graduate from high school. This gives them practical self-defense and confidence training every week. Church activities, youth groups, sports, and musical training all build confidence, which is key to surviving in this world and in making the right decisions. Martial arts classes, with the right instructor, starting at an early age through high school to me is the most important thing you could ever do for your child. However, the ultimate goal is to keep them busy in different activities so they do not have time or energy to be roaming the streets and malls or staying on the computer all night.

out and about: tweens and teens

Girls love to get together with their friends and hang out and talk about boys and clothes and everything else. Your daughter and her friends should be safe as a group if they follow a few simple rules.

The big one: Teach your daughter to never leave her friends behind. Rule #1: If they all go somewhere as a group, they come back as a group—even if they are mad at each other. No exceptions! That

has to be the rule. Period. Use the timing once again, and know where they are.

Rule #2: Girls should never be out-numbered by the guys when they are going somewhere as a mixed group together.

Rule #3: Your children must carry their cell phones, and they must keep them on and answer your calls. Cell phones are a necessity and communication is important. Their cell phones are great tools to help keep them safe.

However, if they have the snazzy new smart phones they want, the new technology brings the same Internet surfing power as a computer to the privacy of their palms. We now have mobile crime happening every day, and even mobile pornography reaching out to your child! Sorry. You were just thinking we had this all figured out, weren't you? The next snag has arrived…

mobile and internet pornography

- In 2005, worldwide revenue from mobile phone pornography was expected to rise to $1 billion and could have grown to three times that number or more within a few years.[9]

- According to IDC, a technology research firm, by the end of 2004, approximately 21 million five- to nineteen-year-olds had wireless phones.[10]

- The mobile adult content market will approach $3.5 billion by 2010, driven by a sharp rise in the adoption of 3G services such as streamed video and video chat, according to a study by Juniper Research.[11]

- The risks to children, particularly teenagers, in cyberspace include exposure to unwanted sexual material (one in three youth) and harassment, threatening or other offensive behavior directed at them (one in eleven youth).[12]

- 31 percent of seventh to twelfth graders pretended to be older to get onto a website.[13]

- Nearly one-third (31 percent) of eight- to eighteen-year-olds have a computer in their bedroom, and one in five (20 percent) have an Internet connection there.[14]

- Three in four (74 percent) young people have a home Internet connection (31 percent have high-speed access). Nearly one-third (31 percent) have a computer in their bedroom, and one in five (20 percent) have an Internet connection there. In a typical day, about half of young people (48 percent) go online from home, 20 percent from school, and 16 percent from someplace else.[15]

- Among the 96 percent of young people who have ever gone online, 65 percent say they go online most often from home, 14 percent from school, 7 percent from a friend's house, and 2 percent from a library or other location.[16]

- The most common recreational activities young people engage in online are playing games and communicating through instant messaging.[17]

- In 2005, one in ten young people (13 percent) reported having a handheld device that connects to the Internet.[18] You can project that it's a much greater percentage now.

So, you can see that it's going to be important to talk through these issues with your kids, and the earlier you start, the easier it's going to be. They need to feel comfortable telling you when something awkward happens, or they see or receive something on their cell phone or e-mail that disturbs them. You can limit or disable their Internet access on their phones and purchase monitoring software. You can even pinpoint their exact location via GPS if it's enabled.

However, while practical, you would be much better off developing a trust relationship with your child and open communications. You don't want them to feel like they have to hide from you or that you're stalking them. Mutual trust is a much better route. But if you feel your child is engaging in dangerous habits or getting themselves involved with unsafe people, do what you have to do to protect

and guide them. After all, they are minors and your responsibility for a reason. They're still kids who are learning their way through the world.

real communication

Teach your children to use their God-given instincts. If they don't feel comfortable around a certain adult or teacher or coach, they need to trust those feelings and tell you about it. If a friend's parents make them uncomfortable, then be more accommodating about having that friend at your house instead of having your child go there. Sure, you don't get the night off, but your kids will remember these things and so will their friends. You never know; you may be giving a child victim the safety and confidence to save themselves or to reach out.

You, as the parent, need to talk about all these things frequently. When I say frequently, I mean daily! Have a new topic every day. Think of different scenarios to cover. For example, suppose there was a big catastrophe and you were separated from your kids. What is your plan to find each other? Your children will enjoy trying to help you solve these scenarios, and you will be surprised how smart they are with the far-fetched answers they come up with that would actually work.

An unusual but effective example: If your daughter finds herself walking in a somewhat secluded area and feels uncomfortable when she sees a group of men at the corner watching her and she doesn't know what to do, tell her to pick her nose, stick her finger down her throat, make herself get sick, or do anything that will make her unattractive to that ill-intentioned group of men. Tweens are a creative group and willing to try about anything, which is why they're great fellow adventurers and also a major risk group for safety. Curiosity and creativity can go either way. It's up to you to guide them safely through these years.

teens

Somewhere in America, a woman is being raped every ninety seconds.

Your daughter is a teenager now. The odds of her being attacked just went up to 69 percent! Wow! Does that scare you? It should. Girls were targeted enough before, but now they are mobile, and more than likely, they have a part-time job as well. So you have to concern yourself with whether they are going to drive safely or get in a car accident from someone else's carelessness or whether they are going to drink and drive, if they are going to talk to the wrong person, if someone is watching them when they leave their job, if they are going to break down on the side of the road, if they are going to let some freak give them a ride, and the list of worries never ends. You can't be everywhere, so you have to make sure your teenager knows how to be aware, make good decisions, and protect himself or herself mentally and somewhat, physically.

out and about: teens

If you have a daughter, talk to her about the way she dresses. I know that most teenage girls like to wear clothes that are rather revealing these days, but you can help her out by teaching her to think a bit defensively and asking her to dress a little more conservatively when she is out alone or will be getting home late. Educate her, Mom and Dad.

On another topic, if your child is old enough to drive, they must know how to change a tire, use jumper cables, and to always have a full tank of gas! If blue lights on a car, appearing to be a police officer, are behind her at night on a desolate road, let her know that she should turn her flashers on and stop only at a well-lit area, preferably in front of a busy restaurant or store. Make sure that she has all of the car doors locked. It is not necessary to roll the window all the way down for a police stop. Just crack it enough to pass through a license and registration. If it is late at night, there is no law that says she cannot ask for a badge number and certification, and she should.

If, in fact, it is a police officer, she should explain that she did not want to stop in a isolated area because she was traveling alone, and she has been taught that attackers often have blue lights installed on their cars to pose as police officers. A real law enforcement agent should expect a woman traveling alone to proceed to the nearest lighted and occupied location before stopping.

Your daughter should, of course, have a cell phone with her and call you or a responsible friend and tell them where she is being stopped. She should stay on the phone with someone the whole time the officer has the vehicle stopped and communicate respectfully. She can also call the police from her cell phone when the blue lights come on and confirm that it is a legitimate police officer stopping her. If it is, she can relay to them that she will stop at the next lit and populated location. This may sound extreme, but it really isn't. It is like everything else, a good, wise safety habit.

dating and partying

To the teens:

Okay, teens. Here is a tough one: dating. Date rape happens more than we know. Sometimes saying, "No" doesn't do it. To reduce the chances of date rape, you have to think ahead a little. For one, it is not necessary to go parking with a guy or go to his house or an unsupervised friend's house when you first start dating, especially at this age. There is no need to go to his house unless you are certain his parents will be there.

Second, I know you are going to party, and your parents know it too, so you and your parents need to talk about underage drinking now. I did. I talked to Hillary over and over again and said that I didn't approve of her drinking underage, but I know I did it at her age, and I drove when I shouldn't have. Hillary knew that if she had been drinking, she could call me at any time to pick her up, and I would not get mad at her, no matter what. However, if she came home and had been drinking and driving, she would lose her driving privileges—for a long time.

Travel in groups and stick together. No one is left behind ever—even if they do want to hook up and are a pain to get home. Here is the most dangerous part about partying with people you kind of know but don't know: getting your drink spiked with a date-rape drug. It is an awful thing to happen, and it happens to someone every day. You wake up, and you know that you have been assaulted, but you do not remember anything. What's worse, you don't know for sure, and you don't know by how many people. If you think this has happened, tell a friend immediately, then go to the local hospital to be examined. This is very important.

Here are a few basics for being out and about. When you are leaving any building late at night, you must do a 360-degree look, twice. When you have to go around a corner, step far away from the corner to be out of the reach of anyone who could be on the other side of the building. In other words, make a really wide turn. If you are approached by someone who makes you uncomfortable, make yourself unattractive, even if you have to stick your finger down your throat and gag or make yourself throw up. This is a major turnoff. No matter what happens, never let yourself be taken to a second location. Fight back! Biting, scratching, and pinching really hurt. Do whatever it takes. Pitch a fit with the same gusto you did when you were two. Kick, scream, bite—you're a lot bigger now, and you'll most likely fight off or deter anyone who tries to take you. Women who fight their attackers typically get away. You're just going to be too much trouble, so the predator will move on.

To the parents:

Parents, if there's a quality reason for your daughter to go to a date's house, make sure the date's parents are home and intend to supervise the date. This is particularly important when you are not very familiar with the young person she is seeing. For example, if she met her date at the mall, how do you know his real age and story? Maybe your daughter even lied about her age just to go out with him. Come on, ladies. We all have lied about our age! Up or down!

Of course, you are going to meet this young man before he takes your daughter out the door, so ask to see his driver's license. This will tell you where he lives and how old he is. If he won't to show it to you, send him out the door—alone. Problem solved before it even started. This is a good resource to share with your daughter as well. She can pre-screen them in the future.

school, authority figures, and backpacks

School should be the one place that you should feel your children are safe, but unfortunately, that is not always the case today. Girls have to be educated about coaches and teachers and other students who may make them feel uncomfortable—for good reason. It happens too often. You see it in the news all of the time—children and teenagers attacked in school or on campus. This can be a risk of continual sexual advances by an authority figure or a straight-out attack. Keep up the quality time you spend with your teen and the depth of communication you maintain so that if a teacher or coach is creating awkward situations for them or directly approaching them about spending private time alone, they feel comfortable telling you about it before opportunity strikes and mistakes are made.

Make sure your children know to be aware of where doors and exits are in any building and to stand near them if they think there could be an issue. If they can, they should keep their backpacks near them where they can be grabbed and used as a weapon or for protection if need be. A twenty-pound bag swinging around will keep most people away or give them a pretty good whack in the head. An issue concerning backpacks is that they should be worn as loosely as possible without the waist strap locked. Why? The number one way a rapist will attack females is from behind by pulling them to the ground by their hair, backpack, or hood of their coats or sweatshirts. Why? So the woman doesn't see them and therefore can't identify them if they happen to find themselves in a lineup.

Does some of this seem like extreme thinking? Paranoia? Well, the reality is that we are all grossly unaware of the real dangers in our society. We have to know that these things happen every minute, and it's our desire not to acknowledge them—and local town's and college's desire to not publicize attacks so they don't scare off visitors and students—that keep us as a society from addressing these enormous problems head on. Until we do, nothing is going to change. Yes, it's the Fight Like a Girl way. Think a little differently than the average person. It is called survival. It is how we're going to make a difference. It is how we're going to stop these monsters from attacking and taking our children and robbing so many of us of our happiness. It is how we're going to save one woman and one child after another from being abused. It's how we're going to take back our lives from fear.

college students

This is when the socially sheltered child can go ballistic with no knowledge of "what lies beneath," if you will. They are on their own; they are all grown-up now. At least, that is what they think. It's up to you, as a parent, to educate your daughter about what she may encounter before she goes to college. Hopefully you have had her in self-defense classes from the time

she was seven or eight until high school graduation! You need to tell her about fraternity parties and how she can easily be taken advantage of at these parties if she doesn't pay attention to her surroundings— especially if she is drinking. Believe me, if she's there long, she probably will be drinking.

I can't tell you how many young women come up to me at Fight Like A Girl seminars and tell me they were sexually assaulted at these types of parties and never reported it or told anyone. They were ashamed because they felt they were to blame for even being there. One of my participants said she screamed, but no one heard her because the music was so loud, even though parents were in the house. Girls, make sure you are never taken to a second location, even at a party. If you are invited to a party, go with some friends. Try to take restroom breaks together. Remember the rule from your tween years—don't ever leave your friend at a party. If you go together, leave together. If one of you has had too much to drink, you can be easily taken advantage of, and that's the truth. Besides, what kind of a friend would you be in the first place if you left your buddy at a party alone just because you wanted to go upstairs and make out with a guy you hardly know?

Just because you might want to risk your safety, doesn't mean your friend does! Do you understand what I mean?

Boy, you ladies are in serious trouble. You are the number one group of victims—ages twenty to twenty-four. A woman is most likely to experience an assault during her first two months of college than any other time. And guess what? He's not hiding in the bushes either. He's someone you know. Every twenty-one hours on each college campus in the United States there is a rape. According to the U.S. Department of Justice, over two-thirds of rapes are committed by someone the victim knows. That's right. 73 percent of sexual assaults are committed by a person who is not a stranger. Guess what? 38 percent of rapists are a friend or an acquaintance of the victim. In addition, according to the FBI, 37 percent of attacks are not even reported.

If you think college campuses are safe, I have news for you. They are not. Do you want to find out how safe colleges are? They are all required by the Jeanne Clery Act to report the crimes that take place on their campuses. So, if you are getting ready to send your son or daughter off to college, you can check their annual crime report thanks to the Crime

Awareness and Campus Security Act of 1990. It was championed by Howard and Connie Clery after their daughter, Jeanne, was murdered at Lehigh University in 1986. Jeanne's parents discovered that students hadn't been told about thirty-eight violent crimes on their daughter's campus in the three years before her murder. They joined with other campus crime victims and persuaded Congress to enact this law. Each school must disclose crime statistics or face a fine of $27,500 by the U.S. Department of Education.[20]

The Department of Justice estimates that 25 percent of college women will be victims of rape or attempted rape before they graduate within a four year period. Also, women between the ages of 16 and 24 will experience rape at a rate that is 4 times higher than the already exorbitant assault rate of all women.[21]

The U.S. Department of Justice has done their homework, and their numbers say to be better prepared and more aware:

1. More then 50 percent of all rapes occurred within one mile of the victim's home or at their home

2.   4 in 10 take place in the victim's home

3.   2 in 10 take place at a home of a friend, neighbor, or relative

4.   1 in 12 take place in parking garages (so avoid parking garages especially between the hours of 6 p.m. and midnight)

5.   43 percent of rapes occur between 6 p.m. and midnight, 24 percent between midnight and 6 a.m., the other 33 percent take place between 6 a.m. and 6 p.m.

Wow, ladies! We really don't stand much of a chance of never having to face this issue, do we? Here are some interesting things that you should know about someone who would commit sexual assault or rape. The average age of a rapist is thirty-one, and guess what? A quarter of them are married, 52 percent of them are white, and in one in three sexual assaults, the rapist was intoxicated or under the influence of some other illegal drug.

Now this part is important, really important! Only 3 percent of rapists used a gun, 6 percent used a knife, and 2 percent used some other form of a weapon. Here's the key: 84 percent used physical force only. So you need to fight back! You can't argue with the U.S. Department of Justice. They have done the research for you, and the statistics are on your side. There is only an 11 percent chance there will be a weapon involved! Even if there is a weapon involved, I would rather die fighting than do what that monster with the weapon wants. Besides, even against a weapon, with the right techniques, you can have the upper hand in less than a second. So, ladies, it is time to be smart and Fight Like A Girl. You can do it! We can make a difference in these statistics.

Here are some suggestions to keep you safe. It's best to start being aware or practicing these things before you go to college and keep it up when you get there—even with all the great distractions.

- Take an intense self-defense class, and not for just a day. For at least several months, enroll in a good martial arts school prior to dating, driving, and college. Let them know that you want to learn self-defense. Parents, go ahead and do this early in life because after they are teenagers, they often think they are invincible and that they know everything.

- Make sure you have a party system in place. That's right! A party plan. Let's face it; you're going to party. Parents, just trust me on this.

- Never go to a fraternity party where males outnumber you. Actually, you should never go anywhere where males outnumber you.

- If your sorority co-hosts a party at a fraternity house, you have to have your wits about you, because their bedrooms are just upstairs! It can be so easy to convince you to go upstairs (I mean, he's so cute and nice), and then no one knows where you are, and the music is so loud that if you do get into trouble no one will hear you! That's the truth.

- Also, never let anyone pour a drink down your throat (beer bongs and keg stands). Don't dive into the trashcan of PJ. You don't know what's been put in there.

- Don't be talked into going to a different location, and if you do want a few minutes alone with Johnny, choose somewhere close by and tell your friends exactly where you're going. That way, if you're not back on time or if something happens, everyone knows where you were and with whom you were talking.

- Never accept a ride home with a stranger. Take a cab or see if the party hosts have a designated driver. If they do, still don't ride with them without a friend. After all, the guy you asked could have just designated himself your driver of the evening.

- Don't walk home alone on campus at night. You can always call campus security and ask them to escort you to your dorm. If you must walk alone at night, call a friend on your cell phone and let them know you're walking and exactly where you are and do not hang up until you are safely in your apartment or dorm. Always have your gal pals with you nearby.

- Take your backpack off to carry in your hand; it can be used to put space between you and your attacker.

- If you have long hair, your hair is your attacker's biggest asset. The number one way that women are attacked is from behind, and if you have a ponytail or long hair, it's so easy to pull you down so you can't even see your attacker. You need to be aware of this and know how to get out of a ponytail pull-down and practice it. This is where your years (or months) of self-defense or Fight Like a Girl classes really pay off—you've already prac-

ticed these things until it's second nature for you to get away.

- If you are going to wear a hooded jacket, then wear the hood up. If you wear it down, it is oh-so-easy for a criminal to grab it and pull the hood down over your eyes and your nose and pull you down from behind. If you already have it on, it's much harder for them to get a hold of it.

- There are guns on campus. I shouldn't have to remind you of the tragedy at Virginia Tech. I am from Virginia, and it broke my heart. But I wasn't surprised that this happened. If someone comes into your class or lab with a gun, grab your desk, your stool, your book bag, or the person next to you and fall to the ground with him or her and play dead. Don't move.

- If you're in a general college class and there are one to three hundred students in there, don't you think if you all decided to rush this guy with the gun, less people would get killed? Of course, someone may get hurt or even die, but there are one to three hundred of you versus one person with a gun! Rush the guy! Remember the recording from the hijacked plane on 9/11? "Let's roll!" Those people made a difference because they stood up together and did

not cower. They saved thousands of lives that day by diverting that one plane.

- In your major department classes, there are what? Fifteen to thirty of you? If one gunman comes in, is it likely that he will be able to shoot everyone if you all decide to beat him like a bad habit all at the same time?

Of course, you have to have thought about these things beforehand and practiced some of them for yourself to have the right reactions in a crisis. That's where Fight Like a Girl seminars and classes come into play and get you prepared for life's surprises.

This is your goal as a Fight Like a Girl team player:

Graduate without being a victim and sometime in your life do something that makes a positive change in this world!

single women

Single! On your own and wide open! Am I right?
Of course I am. I've been there and done that! But
with this designation of being single comes problems. Maybe you have been married for fifteen
years and never got to sow your oats? Maybe your
parents treated you like crap and were so strict, you
never got to experience the things that your friends
did? Now you're like, "Yeah, baby! My time! My
place! I can do what I want, when I want, and I have

no one to clean up after but myself." Now you're invincible!

Being newly single is like being a teenager again. No matter what your age, you think differently, you act differently, and some of your friends are like, "Hey, you need to slow down a little." Guess what? They are probably right. There are people just waiting and watching, hoping you will make a mistake and ask them over, and when you're alone, you don't think about safety so much. Why? Now you're free! Free as a bird! Cheating ex-husband and his girlfriend are out of your life or whatever mess you just escaped. For single women with no kids, here are some things you need to know to keep yourself safe.

home alone

- If you have an alarm on your car, keep your keys with the remote on your nightstand. If you hear something outside or on your porch or have a problem, press the panic button. Let your neighbors know that if your alarm goes off at night, and they don't see you standing there desperately trying to get it off, to look around your house and call the police and come check on you.

- If your home is on the ground level, make sure there are large bushes or plants beneath each window. This will keep someone from being able to approach your window—at least, without making a lot of noise.

- Have houseplants or lamps in front of every ground level window, as this will dissuade potential attackers from entering your home. They can't get in without making a lot of noise before they hit the ground.

- Go to the hardware store and get some of the stick-on window jam and door jam contact alarms. They are really loud, inexpensive, and work very well to scare off potential attackers. You will always know if someone is trying to get in.

- Get a wooden dowel or broomstick cut to the right length, and place it in your sliding glass door for extra protection. Place a tall plant in front of a sliding glass door in a heavy container too. This will make a potential intruder think twice, because it's going to be a lot of trouble to get in quietly.

- Another tip is to make sure there is something you can grab to use as a weapon within two feet of every entry door. It doesn't matter what it is; it could be anything: a stack of hardcover books, a picture in a heavy frame, a vase, a plant, or a radio. What-

ever you can grab to put space between you and an intruder is the key.

- You can keep a steak knife under your pillow, pepper spray on your nightstand, and make sure you have motion lights installed that light up your entryways.

- Get a roommate! Yeah, I know they can be a pain, but like my mom says, safety in numbers! Even if you don't have a roommate, on your answering machine, say, "I'm sorry. We are not here right now. Please leave a message and we will get back to you shortly."

- Fun and practical: Go to my website, www.fightlikeagirl.pro, and watch the video that shows how shopping for shoes can save your life!

working late

If you are someone who works a night shift, guess what? The chances have increased two-fold that someone is watching you, looking to attack. When you are coming to and from work, why not use the buddy system and arrive together with another coworker? Not only will you be safer, but also it will give you both an opportunity to get to know

each other. By doing so, you can make a difference in other people's lives by setting an example for them to follow.

Ask your employer to implement a safe parking area by allocating ten parking spaces for employees close to the entrance of your place of employment. Call it the "Safe Zone." This will do two important things. All of the ladies will now leave their homes earlier to try to get one of those parking spaces, and everyone will notice "who got the parking spaces this time." Before you know it, your employer will be quite happy because now all the women are arriving to work on time. Suppose you are not one of the lucky ten? Guess what? Now you have all the other women arriving in the parking lot at the same time, and you are much less likely to be alone in the dark lot while going to work.

living it up

Yes, you are going to have a drink and do not-so-brilliant things. So, you need to have a support party group! We all need one, don't we? A group of friends that always goes together, and, no matter what, the group never, ever leaves without their party buddies?

That's the rule if you're five or sixty-five. Catching on yet? Even if it makes you or your rather-buzzed buddy mad, it's okay. If the person you're considering throwing caution to the wind for is actually interested in you (or your friend) tonight, then they will be interested tomorrow.

I remember when my best friend, Candice, and I used to go out. We danced all night, had guys buying drinks for us left and right, but somewhere in the scheme of things, somehow our parents, in all of their nagging throughout our lives, got it through our heads that, "Okay, one of us needs to be sober, and we should never leave the other one ever!" Guess what? We did just that. We had a blast and never got in a bad situation simply because we always looked out for each other.

When we weren't close by, we would look across the club and give the thumbs up or down. Thumbs down meant, "This guy is bothering me. Get over here." Hello! It's not that hard, ladies. Set up a buddy system with signals that you can use from across the room. Candice, Debbie, and I survived, and if we did, anybody can! It was all about looking out for each other. It's really not hard, no matter how old you are; just make safety part of your party game plan.

single mothers

Wow, single motherhood. Life can suck, can't it? Now you have to raise yourself and your child. Alone! I know it's not easy, but you can do it, and you both

can survive and thrive and be fine if you have the right attitude. I know; maybe the dad is not in the picture, and maybe your parents aren't either. You have no help and have to go it alone! But, you're not going it alone. You have that precious little person who thinks you're the greatest, and they are going through all of it with you. The one thing that has to keep you going is your child, and guess what? You are keeping them going.

If you're down and upset, they know, and they are upset too. Do you think it's easy being the child of a single parent? Let's look at this both ways. "Ah, poor me. Working all the time and trying to make ends meet." Then think about your child, who misses you so much and just wants to be with you. It's a sad state of affairs, but love and patience will see you through. I hate to add to your stress, but you and your child, particularly, are a major target. A pedophile can easily make his or her way into your life by being sweet and helpful. "Oh, it's okay. I will watch the little princess. You go and have some time to yourself." I know that not everyone is a pervert, but so many are; it's just plain scary! You have to use caution even though you're tired.

Most pedophiles will latch onto single mothers to get to their children, or they will befriend an introverted child from a dysfunctional family. They will either befriend you or try to date you, and in most incidences, you will not know that they are sex offenders. Sexual predators come from all walks of life, all social classes, and all ages. They may shower you and your children with gifts to win your favor. Many predators have hobbies that are child-like, like collecting popular toys, exotic pets, or building plane or car models. These are the kinds of hobbies that are often used to gain a child's trust. These items make a connection with the children, and, therefore, they now look up to the pedophile and think that he or she is safe to be around.

I know it's not fair that just because your ex-husband did you wrong and you divorced him that your child is now a target, but that's the reality. Many pedophiles con the parents and just suck them right in—into a false sense of security because they appear to be "extremely" nice and "extremely" sweet to your kids. Just let me give you some red flags to look out for concerning your kids and their safety from predators.

1. Your newfound adult friend (we will call him John Doe or J.D. for short) would rather focus on your children more than on your own conversation.

2. You have a social function, picnic, BBQ, or whatever, and you find yourself saying, "Oh, isn't J.D. sweet. He has been occupying the children the whole time so I can relax."

3. You think, "Wow. J.D. is just the nicest man I have ever met. Just out of the blue, he brought over some brownies for the kids and me; then he offered to watch the kids for a while so I could have some time to myself."

4. Your kids mention, "Did you know that J.D. has the coolest collection of model cars, robots, and toys?"

Hello! Those are just a few ways your children become targets through you. Just because you're a single parent.

Now, let me tell you why you, ladies, are a target and how you can change your behavior to make a difference.

The number one thing that you can do to save yourself and your kids from a predator is to be aware of your surroundings. Always! No matter how famil-

iar or how many times you have traveled the same sidewalk, pathway, hallway, parking lot, convenience store, or highway home, you have to be continually aware. Your attacker is counting on you being so stagnant in your everyday routine that it will be oh-so-easy to get to you.

Walk with purpose always! No matter how tired you are, act like you are getting ready for the first round in Million Dollar Baby. Even if you are too stubborn to change some things in your daily routine, this is the number one thing that you can do. A would-be attacker will be more likely to attack someone who appears timid and totally oblivious to his or her surroundings.

Here are some more things you can do that can help:

- Find a female friend you can trust to watch your kids when necessary. Statistically, female pedophiles are rare. If she is a single mom too, great! You both can feel each other's pain and joys and take turns keeping the kids. Just make sure that there are no boyfriends or estranged ex-husbands that will be watching your child in your friend's absence.

- Get involved in an organization working with kids and single moms like you. Networking will help you get through the tough times. You know, angels aren't just in heaven. They are all around us. God places people around us each day that can help us if the need arises. We just need to know that it's okay to ask for help. God will send help, and he will send it in the strangest forms that you can imagine! Trust me. I have been like, "God, this is my help? Umm, okay," and it has worked out better than I could have planned every time.

- Never have a male friend-of-a-friend watch your child. Ever.

- Your child goes with you or a trusted female, period, or you just don't go out. I am sorry, but there is someone else more important in your life: your child—not you. These are the sacrifices you make as a parent, and you get the joys in return. That's why I love my parents so much. I know how hard they worked to make my brother and me happy. I am so blessed to know both of my parents. So many kids do not. So if you're the only parent, then be the best! Make cookies with your kid, take a walk, play ball, or just color. It doesn't matter. All they want is for you to notice them and give them a little of your time. Do that, and you will just be fine.

- Let's say that your child wants to go to a friend's house down the street and stay. Do you know the parents? What do they do? How many kids do they have? How long have they lived there? Why did they move here? If you get to know them and feel comfortable with letting your child go down the street on their own to their friend's house, then you need to go with them the first time. Time the trip and see how long it takes to get there. Then from that moment on, they have to call you in exactly that amount of time. If the phone isn't ringing saying they are there safe, then they are grounded and have to come home or you have to go get them. Be steadfast on this policy. It's going to be trying at first, but once they get in the habit, it will be a safe one that you can pass on to other parents.

Home Alone. Single moms, in this case, you're the same as single women, except with precious babies to protect. Read the Home Alone part of the Single Women's section just before this so you'll know how to prevent intruders in your home.

female executives

There used to be a time in America when a woman being in charge of a major corporation was a big joke. Well, not anymore. Today, women are running those companies, and with the responsibility of running a major corporation comes more complications. The one thing that I do like about female executives is that they definitely have the keyword that I preach about at all my seminars: awareness. That is how they got where they are today. They are very in tune to what's going on around them and what they can do to make it better. That's the key to success in life and success in being safe. Here are some of the things that you may have to deal with on a daily basis as a female executive:

1. Jealously from the men and the women who got passed over for the job you have.

2. Balancing family and career, which is very difficult, especially if you are making more than your mate. At first it may be okay, but then resentment often sets in because you have become a prominent figure, and it makes your mate feel insignificant. Too often, you end up single again.

3. Being approached constantly by people who want your time, mainly for their own personal gain. Be cautious of people who are in your inner circle at your corporation. Among them is usually someone who wants to see you fail.

4. Knowing whom to trust. More often than not, the poor, single mom who sits at her desk every morning, gets you coffee and is always there to help because she needs her job is the one who is loyal. Perhaps she's the one you should promote?

5. Dealing with loneliness. It's lonely at the top. That is the price so many women pay for success. Unfortunately, on the way up the career ladder, you will lose a lot of friends, husbands, boyfriends, and

more, not because you're difficult, but because you have no time for them.

6. Spending late hours in the office and finishing up contracts and obligations that just can't wait is what made you a CEO. But remember when you leave, even though you have been putting up with employees all day, you had to fire someone today, you had to get the new budgets done, and everything else on your normal schedule, you still have to keep your guard up. Here's your number one liability and asset. You are one of the most aware people around. You are in tune to everything all day! However, it's like a release when you leave and head for your car to go home. Your awareness drops because you have been on guard and intent all day. I'm right, aren't I? Do me a favor and keep your head focused until you are safely in your house.

7. Handling people who work for you outside the office—personal trainers, cooks, maids, drivers, gardeners, pet sitters, nannies… Be nice, but be careful if you ever feel uncomfortable in your own home with someone. Follow your instincts. So many women think that just because they are wealthy, nothing will happen to them. Wrong! If a predator can get to you, you're the first person they would come after—looks, flash, money, jewelry, the works. Spend the money on a bodyguard or real

self-defense classes. You can get private lessons that fit your schedule. Invest in learning something that can save your life or someone else's.

8. Managing your image for safety. Just because you have them, does not mean you need to walk around wearing a fortune in clothing and jewelry. It's much safer for you to dress down—way down. This will make you less of a target. Instead of taking the Bentley out shopping, get something not so flashy. Maybe a Jeep or something that shows signs of independence and strong will. Really, think about it. Would you mess with a woman wearing black leather on a Harley? She could be anyone—a CEO like you, a lawyer, a doctor, or a drifter. It doesn't matter because the image is going to make a predator think twice about bothering her. They say you can't judge a book by the cover, but we all do. So make the cover someone who's less of a target.

the totally oblivious

I have touched on this quite a bit already, but I have to touch on it in more depth. Who are the totally oblivious? Typically, anyone who falls into these categories: twelve to seventeen-year-olds, eighteen to twenty-four year olds, and I call the other category "Divas."

If your child is between the ages of twelve and seventeen, you already know that they think they know everything and you don't know anything. From the time your child turns twelve, the statistics are not in their favor. You have act to overcome them. If you do nothing, they're in serious trouble. If your child is between the ages of sixteen and nineteen, they are four times more likely to be a victim of rape. Here are the characteristics of someone who is totally oblivious and setting themselves up for attack:

Someone who...

- walks around late at night, going to the convenience store while texting or talking on the phone.

- hangs out on the street between midnight and 6 a.m.

- lets their child walk home from a friend's house rather than going to pick them up or walk with them.

- parks in parking garages and doesn't take the time to park in a good spot with light. They don't consider that when they leave the mall or airport or office late, it will be dark, and they park in a faraway corner.

- walks around with music playing in their ears all the time, looking down or studying their phone, never

seeing who's watching them while they're being oblivious.

- walks around corners without giving a thought to who or what may be on the other side and never looking or leaving distance between themselves and the unknown.

- gets drunk and then does anything in public without a trusted friend who is responsible for their safety.

- goes off in private with someone they just met.

If you recognize yourself as a totally oblivious person, this whole book is for you. Start with the toddlers and work your way up. Seriously. You can benefit from every tip. A few little hints to get you started:

- If it's dark when you have finished your work shift, and you have to walk to your car, either as a teen or an adult, call someone on your phone as you are leaving. Let them know you are on the way to your car, and keep them on the line but look around as you talk. If you see someone suspicious, talk about how your friend is just around the corner and you'll see them in a second. You can fake talking to someone if you need to, but just as you step out of the elevator or into the parking lot, make sure you're

looking around, have your car keys ready, and, most importantly, take a good look in and around your car. I mean a good look.

- If you're in a shopping center lot, when you leave, grab a shopping cart and keep it in from of you. Look around, and if you need to, you can use the cart to keep space between you and a potential attacker.

- You know those little pop-out umbrellas that seem to show up as gifts? Well, if you generally work late or in a bad neighborhood, carry one with you. You can just pop the button and that thing will explode and keep space between you and a potential attacker.

- If you're a diva, I know you want to be fashionable, but if you can't run in your shoes or slip them off quickly enough to throw at somebody, then you don't need to dress like a streetwalker! Yes, it's a free country, but the more skimpy clothing you wear, the more the guys check you out. I understand that this is the point, but late at night, after a potential rapist has consumed way too many alcoholic drinks, is not the time for you to be walking around alone half dressed. If you want to dress that way with your boyfriend or partying with a trusted group of friends, then just stay together…and try not to cause your boyfriend too much trouble. A little hint: layer your look and accessorize with belts or complicated zippers and buttons. You can pull off sexy and difficult to get to at the same time! A predator doesn't want to go to a lot of trouble, so make your look chic but complex.

Are you getting the picture? I hope so, because I don't want to see you get hurt just because you're totally oblivious. Try to make a change in your awareness, and if you believe that scatter-brained is your natural personality, then balance it out by being the best escapist you can be. Treat yourself to as many lessons in escape techniques as it takes to make you proficient. At least then, when you are in a challenging situation or someone grabs you, you can be out and gone in two seconds or less. Really!

current stalking victims

According to the National Center for Victims of Crime, the definition of stalking is, "A course of conduct directed at a specific person that would cause a reasonable person to feel fear." Stalking can escalate over time. Three in four stalking victims are stalked by someone they know. However, someone you don't know can stalk you. Years ago, I was stalked, and I really wasn't sure who was doing it. It scared my family and me.

Finally, I had my dad come over and wait for the stalker's call and when he did, my dad gave him some choice words, something along the lines of, "Stay away from my daughter, or you will be pushing up daisies." My dad also took steps to reinforce my home with extra locks and sticks in the sliding glass door, plants in front of the sliding door, and lawn furniture on the back deck that would have to be moved to gain entry to the back of the house. Finally, the person went away. But that wasn't the last time I was stalked. It happened two other times in my life, but by then I was so in tune to self-defense and had my own karate studio, so I picked up on it immediately and put an end to it.

Sometimes, admiration will turn into stalking. People will put you on a pedestal and just want to be your friend. Often, when someone breaks up with another person, rejection sets in, and stalking can start from that as well. This can happen even between husbands and wives, boyfriends and girlfriends…

For example, your husband or boyfriend doesn't pay any attention to you, won't do anything with you,

and always finds something wrong with everything you do. So, you cheat on him. Stupid, but someone was appreciating and paying attention to you and he wasn't. You are really devastated by what happened and truly sorry for your mistake, but no matter what you do, he just won't speak to you. You try and try, but you aren't making any progress. He breaks up with you, but you still want to make amends. You want to know what's going on with your ex, so you keep pursuing contact with him; but that can easily turn into stalking, so be careful.

If you find yourself in that situation, a little advice: express your guilt, and if he really knows that he was not paying any attention to you and was actually part of the problem, he will eventually come around if you aren't obsessively stalking him. If he doesn't, then he may just be a selfish, self-centered, and unforgiving person. If that's the case, move on, and let it go. Don't get yourself in trouble trying to be the nice guy or girl. Sometimes that will get you in trouble. The same thing can happen in reverse as well, and you end up with a husband or boyfriend stalking you all the time.

Being stalked can happen to anyone, for any reason. Be aware and try to put an end to it before your stalker takes stronger and stronger action. Just think about the movie Fatal Attraction. That woman still scares me! Here are some of the things that stalkers will do, according to the National Center for Victims of Crime.[22]

- Follow you and show up wherever you are.

- Send unwanted gifts, letters, cards, or e-mails.

- Damage your home, car, or other property.

- Monitor your phone calls or computer use.

- Use technology, like hidden cameras or global positioning systems (GPS), to track where you go.

- Drive by or hang out at your home, school, or work.

- Threaten to hurt you, your family, friends, or pets.

- Find out about you by using public records or online search services, hiring investigators, going through your garbage, or contacting friends, family, neighbors, or coworkers.

- Posting information or spreading rumors about you on the Internet, in a public place, or by word of mouth.

- Other actions that control, track, or frighten you.

- Use technology such as e-mail or instant messaging to bombard you with contact.

Being stalked can affect you at work too. One in eight employed stalking victims lose time from work as a result of their victimization and lose five days of work or more. If you are being stalked, it is very important that you let your employer know. So many times, estranged people or strangers will actually come to your place of employment. This is not good, because eventually something is going to happen. So it is very important that you let your employer and fellow employees know what's going on. If you are being stalked, it will affect your health. Constant fear of not knowing what is going to happen next and continual fear for yourself, your family and pets, or your property will take its toll. Stalking is serious. Why? Because 67 percent of the women that are killed as a result of stalking were killed by an intimate partner who had already abused them.

This next statistic is really scary. Eighty-nine percent of women murdered who had been physically assaulted were also stalked the twelve months prior to their murder. Of stalking victims who did report their predicament to the police, 54 percent were killed anyway. [23]

So what can you do? Stalking is unpredictable and dangerous. No two stalking situations are alike. There are no guarantees that what works for one person will work for another, yet you can take steps to increase your safety.

- Change the locks and deadbolts in all your doors.

- If you are in immediate danger, call 911.

- Trust your instincts. Don't downplay the danger. If you feel you are unsafe, you probably are. If this person is threatening you, your dog, your cat, your family members, then guess what? It's safe to say they are dangerous.

- Take threats seriously. Danger generally is higher when the stalker talks about suicide or murder when a victim tries to leave or end the relationship.

- Contact a crisis hotline, victim services agency, or a domestic violence or rape crisis program. They can help you devise a safety plan, give you information about local laws, weigh options such as seeking a protection order, and refer you to other services.

- Develop a safety plan, including things like changing your routine, arranging a place to stay, and having a friend or relative go places with you. Also, decide in advance what to do if the stalker shows up at your home, work, school, or somewhere else. Tell people how they can help you.

- Don't communicate with the stalker or respond to attempts to contact you.

- Get a restraining order. You are letting the police know what's going on.

- Get a great security system, motion lights, a loud dog, etc.

- Ask to borrow a friend or family member's car. If you can, change out or trade cars with someone on a regular basis. If they know you are being stalked, they will be more than glad to help, and if your stalker still manages to follow you while you are in someone else's car, the situation is very serious, and you need to make bigger changes.

- Start staying with a friend or get a roommate. Ask friends if they will stay over with you.

- If you can't afford a security system, make sure you have bushes under your windows—something thorny (i.e. rose bush or pyracantha bush that is

very pretty but can cause a major problem if someone is trying to climb in through a window). Go to the hardware store and purchase stick-on contact alarms for all your windows and your doors. They are inexpensive, very loud, and easy to install.

- Secure all windows and sliding glass doors with a wooden stick.

- Keep plants, lamps, or furniture in front of windows or doors.

- Purchase a garden sprayer, fill it with nail polish remover, and keep it by your bed. This is an extreme eye irritant that you can spray in an attacker's face.

- Keep a knife under your pillow.

- Make sure there is something you can reach in every room to use for protection to put space between you and an attacker.

- Keep your car keys by your nightstand and use the remote (if you hear something) to set off your car alarm. You can also get an extra stick-on contact alarm and keep it by your bed to make a loud noise if you need it.

- Let your neighbors know what's going on and to be on the lookout for this person or anything that looks suspicious.

- Change your cell number and get a new e-mail address.

domestic violence victims

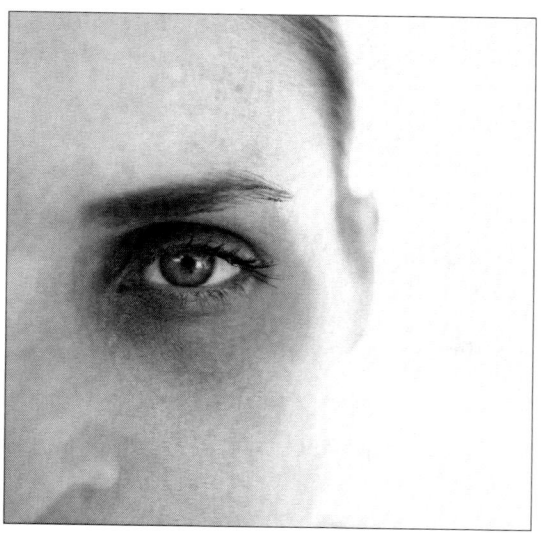

Of course, this is the statement I hate to hear from someone on a Hotline call or seeking information from of my social worker buds at domestic abuse shelters: "But I can't stay here. I am not one of those people." This typically comes from a well-to-do woman and her child who left her wealthy husband to seek help. She's usually been beaten horribly, but yet she does not want to stay at the shelter where it is safe. How is it possible that a woman who is highly educated, has a great career and her own resources would stay in a relationship with someone who beats her and her child? How can a man be considered a pillar of the community when he beats his wife and children on a regular basis?

Domestic violence crosses every socioeconomic boundary. Every two in three female victims are related to their attacker. There are, of course, always many more unreported numbers that are not included in statistics that drive the actual numbers even higher! Particularly in same-sex relationships, when abuse occurs and is reported, officers do not know the relationship between the people involved, or they elect to not list it as domestic violence. Most domestic violence between gays and lesbians end up classified as "assault" or "battery," making it almost impossible to get the correct statistics on the issue with same-sex abuse.

Most shelters cater to women and children, and a lot of gays and lesbians feel that there are not enough facilities that can help them, or they don't fit in and really don't know where to go. Hello,

everyone! The shelters are for men, women, and children—no matter how rich or poor you are or what your situation. If you are in trouble, go. They will point you in the right direction and really want to help, no matter what your relationship or gender or social status. Besides, assisting you with discretion and privacy is their specialty.

So, how do you know if someone is being abused? As I said, abuse crosses every socioeconomic boundary and relationship type. Your friend may have bruises frequently. Usually, if they have a black eye, that's their abusers way of keeping them at home or isolated. I will tell you now that I am a former victim turned self-defense expert and world karate champion. It's hard to get a black eye. You have to get hit really hard and precisely around the eye. So if your friend comes to work more than once with a black eye, guess what? They can make up all the excuses they want. Unless they have had some recent eye surgery, somebody probably hit them.

If they are wearing long sleeves in the midst of a sweltering summer, they are probably bruised on their arms. They will not be as out-going anymore; they'll have lower self-esteem and avoid any kind of confrontation whatsoever. If they are constantly walking on eggshells at home with their abuser, they'll be doing it around you too. It's easier to act a certain way than to get hit again. As your friend talks about home life, if they constantly say, "Well, it was my fault," they are certainly being emotionally abused.

Isolation is the key to controlling a domestic violence victim. They will have limited use of the telephone, an inability to access funds, limited ability to go out alone, and if invited somewhere, they have to always bring their partner. Domestic violence needs to stop and stop now. You are not helping yourself, your children, or your family by staying in an abusive situation. Corporations lose billions of dollars each and every year as a result of violence at home. Employees lose time and productivity from work, accumulate medical bills that are covered by company health insurance, and generally can't focus on the job they are being paid to do because their life is so stressful. This problem is also a worldwide financial problem; billions are lost and millions are hurt. Together we can change the statistics.

telltale signs that you need to stop it now

There are red flags to alert you to a potentially abusive or unstable person in your life. We'll look at a few things that should put you on guard and a few ways to monitor early interactions.

First thing, your mom was right. If someone seems too good to be true, then guess what? They are. Let me tell you something. If you cannot find one flaw with this person—their pants are perfectly creased, their hair is perfect, their nails are manicured, and their story is fairy-tale ideal—there's probably something they're hiding or you aren't seeing. Don't get me wrong. There is nothing wrong with looking good, but if they seem too obsessed about every

detail of their presentation, there's something missing in them.

Here is a simple test to try the theory: if you're out with Mr. Perfect, accidentally spill something on him at the dinner table and see what his reaction is. I am serious. Do it. How did he react? Body language and words will teach you a lot. If his reaction is violent or excessive in proportion to the incident, you'll know what you have to look forward to in your relationship.

Abusive people may be charming beyond belief, taking you to expensive restaurants and showering you with gifts that they may not be able to afford. They may tell you how gorgeous you are at first and then further into the relationship shift to explaining how great they are. They may start trying to control you by being abrasive when you spend time with your friends. For example, let's say you bowl every Tuesday night, and you have been doing this since long before you met him. All of a sudden, he will plan a date or make reservations at a nice restaurant that same night. If you say, "But tonight's my bowling night" (this is where the guilt trip comes in), they will say, "Well, I thought you would like to go to this restaurant. It was hard to get reservations. Can't you leave your bowling buddies for just one night, or do they mean more to you than I do?" Guess what? If you go to that restaurant, they are already closing in on you. Little plans you have that get manipulated and isolate you from people who care about you will rapidly grow into larger power plays.

Emotionally abusive people have to feel they are in control, and it starts in little doses that get bigger and bigger. Once they start blocking your friends out of your life, then they will start isolating you from your family. They may give you a hard time about going to family functions, saying, "They're stupid; you should stay here with me." This will escalate to their being extremely jealous of anybody and everybody who has anything to do with you. At this point, you are in the relationship pretty deeply already. I'd say at least to your hips! Here is the kicker. By this time, they are jealous of everyone but tell you that no one else would ever have you. However, it is okay if their eyes wander because they are the greatest. Everyone wants them, by the way.

This is how it starts, and from here, ladies, it doesn't stop unless you make a conscious effort to get away. If you are in a situation like this, be confident that it will only get worse. Your partner will soon be controlling everything about you and your actions until you make it stop. If you're in a physically abusive relationship, here are some helpful hints. Leave! If you won't do that immediately, learn how to defend yourself physically, as quickly as possible. Keep a good first-aid kit handy. If you are not going to leave soon, invest in a life insurance policy on yourself benefitting your kids or your parents, because the fact is that according to the Federal Occupational Safety and Health Administration, in 2003 the second leading cause of death for women on the job was murder by an estranged boyfriend or husband.

Start saving money for yourself or your kids (if you have them), because you will all need therapy after witnessing and dealing with abuse for years. You also need to make plans for people to care for your children in the event that something does happen to take you out of commission. Seriously! I refuse to sugarcoat anything as serious as this. Wake up! Stand up! Get out! You can do it. Thousands of women do and live to tell about it. Don't be a statistic! There are too many to list, but here are some key points below:

The facts:

- 77 million women and children are assaulted each year![1]

- 2000 kids are reported missing every day![2]

- One in four U.S. women (25 percent) has experienced domestic violence in their lifetime.[3]

- Between 600,000 and 6 million women are victims of domestic violence each year, and between 100,000 and 6 million men.[4]

- In 2001, three out of four homicide victims who were murdered by their partners were women.

Homicide was the second leading cause of death for women on the job in 2003.[5]

- 44 percent of female domestic violence victims are left without transportation because the abuser disabled the vehicle or hid the keys.[6]

- Women account for 85 percent of victims of intimate partner violence; men account for 15 percent.[7]

- Intimate partner violence affects people regardless of income. However, people with lower annual income (below $25K) are at a three-times higher risk of intimate partner violence.[8]

- Studies show that access to shelter services leads to a 60- to 70-percent reduction in incidence and severity of reassault during the three to twelve months following the assault.[9]

- 74 percent of Americans personally know someone who is or has been a victim.[10]

- More than three women and one man are murdered by their intimate partners in this country every day.[11]

Part Two:

GETTING OUT OF A BAD SITUATION

what do you do now?

Let's say you are already in an abusive relationship, whether it's a boyfriend, girlfriend, husband, or partner. How do you make a change? How do you get out? What can you do? Where do you begin?

The good news is that you have bought this book, and you are acknowledging that this isn't right. Hopefully, you are determining that you don't want to take it anymore. You may have left before but went back. Maybe you believed some of these reasons and excuses:

9. "I'm never going to hit you again. I am so sorry. Please come back," they say as they shower you with gifts and maybe even shed a tear or two.

10. "I just can't live without you. If you don't come back to me, I will kill myself, and it will be your fault," and you believed that might be true.

11. "I'll kill you if you leave or tell anyone about this," or "I'll get full custody of the kids if you leave because you won't be able to support them."

12. "You can't make it financially. With the kids, starting over will be too hard."

So you told yourself that they would change this time, and they didn't. Don't be surprised. All of these are trademark reasons and excuses, and you have to know that abusive people rarely change. Even if they're going to, you don't deserve to live through their practice years. You have to make a plan to free yourself and your children, if you have them, before any or more truly violent acts happen and more emotional damage is done in your life and the lives of those you love.

If you have children, it is your responsibility to protect them—emotionally and physically—to the best of your ability. So, I'm showing you how to increase your ability. Determine to act.

You will need two courses of action: Plan A and Plan B. For every step, choose two options that will work best for you. Plan A and Plan B. Make sure you have someone to help you carry out the plans. You should not do this on your own. You will need help. Right now, even though you are reading this, you are still passive, and your self-esteem is nearly gone. You will need someone, a family member, a close friend or coworker, who knows how to follow through, to support you in your escape. This is the first step.

Step one: People. Identify the people who are going to help you.

- Option one: Locate the nearest women's shelter in your area. Make sure this is the first thing that you do before you plan anything. They can help you obtain legal assistance and tell you what your options are. They can also provide you with information concerning your children and custody issues. Shelter workers can inform you about restraining orders and tell you how to start that process as well. They're there to help you make a new start.

- Option two: If there is no shelter in your area, is there a family member you can trust who will help you?

- Option three: If you have no family nearby or family that can come to help you, is there a friend, coworker, social worker, or pastor in whom you could confide?

Stop making excuses! You do know someone who will help you.

Step two: Tell. Once you've identified who you'd like to help you, tell them what has been happening, and let them know that you want to make a plan to get away from your abusive partner safely. Once they've agreed to help, make sure you are very clear about what you need them to do and when and where.

Step three: Plan. I am sure that there is something you do on a routine basis alone or with the kids, if you have children, like getting the groceries, picking up the kids from school or a practice, visiting a friend, etc. You need to plan the exact day when you are going to leave and set that goal and stick to it. If you have children, you may want to plan for them to be at a friend or family member's house where you can pick them up after you've left home to prevent a possible conflict or delay. If you truly believe you have to leave while your partner is at home, take a look around the house and eliminate as many things as possible that he could use to hurt you or to stop you. Start preparing now for everything that could happen.

Step four: Lodging. You have to go somewhere that you will be safe. You can't count on not being found by your abuser. A place that you would never pick in a million years is where you will be safe! Make sure you think like the person you want to be, not like the predictable person you have been.

- Option one: Unknown Territory. If you have the means to hire personal protection for you and your kids, this is the time to do it. You can go to a hotel, rental home of an acquaintance, rent a condo or apartment, and have your bodyguard ensure that you are safe. Remember not to use credit or debit cards that your partner can access, or they will

know from your charges where you are. Families of all socio-economic situations are affected by violence and abuse. If you have the resources, siphon off enough cash before leaving to hire protection and acquire a place to stay that is unknown to your partner.

- Option two: Shelter. If there's a women's shelter in your area, this can be a good option because you'll have knowledgeable support and security. If you feel your life may be in danger, this may be your best option as there are experienced people there to help and protect you, and they can help you get protection from the legal system and the authorities as quickly as possible. If you have children in school, you'll want to get legal protection immediately before letting them out of your sight.

- Option three: Family. This may be the first place your partner looks, so, if possible, choose a family member he does not know well or one with lots of people in the household, preferably large guys. If you have children, it may be helpful for them to be close to familiar faces during this turbulent time. Should you find yourself in a custody hearing later, it's also very understandable that you would escape to a family member's home for protection, provided that it is a safe environment. If your family lives out of town and you can get there reliably, this may be your best option. However, check your legal standing and rights before taking children out of the state, and be very certain of them if you're considering leaving the country.

- Option four: Friends. If you have friends who can offer a safe haven for you, this may be a good short-term solution. Make sure, especially if you have children, that you make wise decisions about what is a suitable environment. If you have any other options, don't take yourself or your children to places that a court could consider questionable. Remember, you are making a fresh start. Make it a clean one. If you have friends out of town, this may be a good choice. Again, make sure of your legal rights concerning your children if you're crossing state lines or leaving the country.

- Option five: Other properties. Even if you have other homes, apartments, rental units, or can rent a house, an apartment, or a hotel room, you should only go somewhere like this if you have people with you for physical protection at all times. Hotel and apartment doormen are not sufficient protections. Your once-charming, abusive partner will get past them with ease. These are options you may want to consider after you have legal protection and feel the situation has settled down considerably.

Step five: Money. You will need cash. Estimate how much you will need to get as far away as you can. Start stashing money away every day. Five dollars here, ten dollars there. When you get groceries, you can squeeze extra cash by purchasing more pasta or items on sale. Funnel the savings into your escape pile. You will have to hide it somewhere where your partner will never look in a million years like a tampon box or inside a cosmetics bag. Sometimes there is an obvious object that's right in the open that no one every pays any attention to such as a kitchen item or a cookbook. Everyone has one they never open. Those are just a couple of ideas. Do whatever you can to have some cash, because you can be tracked by credit card charges. If your partner is violent, he will try to find you. Cash leaves no paper trail.

Step six: Transportation. Planes, trains, and automobiles. Buses and bikes. Anything will do as long as it's reliable and will get you where you need to go—faster than your partner could if he decided to chase you and knew where to look. Make sure you have a backup plan for every step.

- Option one: If you have your own car or one you use, you must make sure it is in great running condition. If it isn't, choose another option. If you do have access to your own car or even his, make sure you have two extra sets of keys made. If you're using your own car and must leave while he is at home, make sure you disable his. Flatten the tires on the blind side of the car or remove the coil wire or something you're certain will stop it from running.

- Option two: If he drives the only car, just remember that you do know someone who can help you. You may be able to borrow a car from a friend to help you make your escape.

- Option three: You may be able to rent a car and drive away from the rental shop, or rent it the day before and have it parked nearby, waiting for the time you are scheduled to leave.

- Option four: You may need to have someone pick you up, either at home or somewhere you can be. God works through people he has put on this earth. There are angels all around you that are willing and able to help you if you are just bold enough to ask. If you have a friend that is going to help you get away, have a backup person as well.

- Option five: You may be able to use public transportation or a taxi to make your escape. Just make sure

you aren't going somewhere your partner would ever guess or could beat you to, so he can't be there waiting for you when you arrive.

Step seven: Contacts. If you don't have a cell phone, get one. Buy or borrow one. You can get a prepaid card phone if you don't want a service plan. Make sure anyone helping you has a cell phone, and you have their numbers saved in your phone and written in several places. Have the police phone number on speed dial, and remember 911 is for any emergency. This is very important. You already know what your partner is capable of and how things could escalate if he catches you leaving. You have to be prepared for the worst and hope for the best.

Step eight: Gather. Get something for protection: pepper spray, mace, or a stun gun. Have your driver's license, passport, birth certificate, other photo IDs, credit cards, gas cards, and cash together in your purse or a small bag. If you have kids, put their birth certificates, recent school records, photo IDs, and dental records with your papers as well. If you have a car, make sure you have the registration and insurance card and title, if you have it.

If you're going to be able to leave when your partner is away, you can pack a bag with clothes and toiletries and shoes. You can do this very slowly. First, get the piece of luggage for yourself and your kids. Take it somewhere other than your house and leave it empty. Pick it up the day you leave. You're going to use large black garbage bags to pack. Why? Because if you tie them up, they look like garbage, and you can throw them in your car and take out the trash. Place a trashcan near your washing machine with a black garbage bag in it. Every time you do laundry, stow something in the bag for you and your kids a little at a time. Take it to where your luggage is stored. He can't be around every minute. Everyone does laundry, so this is a great way to get ready. If you're going to be looking for a new job, keep that in mind as you pack. If you have kids, toward the end of your packing (because kids notice their things missing) put some clothes and favorite toys and important schoolbooks or projects they're working on in a bag as well. Pack light, but get the essentials.

Important: During this process and as your escape plays out, your kids should not have access to their phones or yours, except in your presence. This is not a regular separation. It's a violent, abusive situation, and you are escaping to save your-self and your kids. However, the abuser is still their parent, and they still love them. Even though they may hate what happens to you and to them, physically and emotionally, it's all they know.

Normal is what you know, and it would be very easy for the abuser to charm his way into finding out where you are. Until things have calmed down and you have a solid protection in place for you and the kids, you must be clear about this with your children and sleep with your cell phone under your pillow so they can't sneak it from you.

Step nine: Leaving. Your time has come. Be strong and courageous. You can hold your head up. You're making your move to a better life.

- Option one: Ideally, you can just choose a time your partner is out of town or out of the house for a while (gone to work, fishing, at a sports event, on a trip, etc.) and leave with the kids and be gone.

- Option two: If you go to work, that's a great time to make your move. You won't be expected home for hours, and you most likely have childcare arranged, so you could pick them up without incident and leave.

- Option three: Most likely, you go out without him for regular errands or chores, and you could take the kids (if you are certain you can convince them to get in the car without a lot of questions or resistance) or pick them up from another location and leave without incident.

- Option four: If you truly have no freedom, and you must leave while your partner is in the house, you could crush up some sleeping pills and mix them in his meal. This will hopefully put him to sleep and give you the opportunity that you need to get away. It's very important to make sure that you give him only the recommended dose. You don't want to end up in prison for an overdose. That will not help you or your family at all!

You must prepare yourself with excuses and backup plans and be ready for the extreme. Consider the "what ifs…" What if he catches you leaving? What if he gets up and grabs one of the kids? What if you can't get the kids to get in the car? Think of a story and scenario for every step of your plan and a way to get it done. Have other people help you. They'll be

your biggest deterrent to violence, especially if your partner doesn't want anyone to think he's abusive. If you have witnesses, anything negative he does can be used against him—and in your favor—later.

Step ten: Make sure you start taking steps to become financially independent if you aren't already. I realize this may be really hard for you, but there are so many options available to you now in the work force—many just for women and especially for mothers. Many companies have created flextime, have on-site childcare, and also have telecommuting options so you can work from home. Companies are finally getting it!

A lot of people can do their jobs via telecommuting (working for the company via computer and phone from home). Your best resource to find out about jobs for the working mom is Working Mother Magazine. Besides providing a lot of important information, every year they publish the "Working Mother 100 Best Companies" review. Strong companies fight to make this list each year by providing better work options and environments for working moms. You can check out one hundred great companies for working mothers in this year's list on the Internet at www.workingmother.com.

you have defenses

The Federal Occupational Safety and Health Administration has begun to more aggressively punish employers who fail to take steps to protect employees from the dangers of workplace violence. If you are being stalked by an estranged intimate partner, let your employer know immediately. As we mentioned before, homicide was the second leading cause of death for women on the job in 2003.[1]

one: legal defenses

It's important to know where to get legal help. If there is not a shelter in your area, keep this number handy. The National Domestic Violence Hotline is 1.800.799.SAFE, and this website (www.abanet.org)

explains to you in an easy and understandable way your legal rights and legal steps that you can take to protect yourself and your children. It is a great resource. I have listed their suggestions below to help you better understand what you need to do. Remember, domestic violence is against the law! It is a crime in all states, although each state's laws are a little different. According to the American Bar Association, domestic violence can be handled in three different courts. Below are some facts and helpful information regarding your legal rights.

- Criminal court is where the state will prosecute the abuser. Possible crimes include abuse of an intimate partner, violation of a protective order, elder abuse, child abuse, murder, rape, assault, kidnapping, false imprisonment, property destruction, vandalism, trespassing, stalking, unlawful possession or concealment of a weapon, intimidating a witness, and many others.

- Civil court is where you might address violation of a protection order or sue for money damages. Possible civil lawsuits include sexual harassment, personal injury, and others.

- Divorce or family court is where family violence directly affects divorce proceedings and can be a factor in limiting or prohibiting the abuser's rights to child custody or visitation privileges.

- Domestic violence might also involve child abuse and neglect and might impact other areas of law, such as public benefits and immigration status.

- A Court Order of Protection is your fastest form of legal help. A Court Order of Protection is an official legal notice, enforceable in court, that requires the abuser to stop the violence and abuse. Relief available under a Court Order of Protection can be tailored to your specific needs and can address your concerns. It can order the abuser to stay away from you and can prevent him from contacting you by phone, mail, text, e-mail, fax, or through third parties. It can force the abuser to move out of your home and give you exclusive use of the car. The court may award temporary custody of children to you, along with child support, spousal support, and the continuance of insurance coverage. The police can arrest and jail the abuser for violating the order.

- To get a Court Order of Protection, call the local state or district attorney or tell your local police that you need to get one. They will tell you whom

to contact. You will have to go to court. In court, you will have to convince the judge that you or your children have been threatened with violence or that you have suffered abuse. Witnesses, including police officers, can help your case. Depending on your state law and how the court applies it, physical evidence is also helpful but not essential. Physical evidence could include signs of physical abuse such as bruises and photos of physical damage to property or objects used in the assault.

- For a Court Order of Protection to work, it should focus on your specific safety needs. If you have children and are concerned for their safety, you must specifically request custody and visitation restrictions or "no contact" orders. You must call police every time the order is violated. You should make lots of copies of the protection order and carry a copy with you everywhere, especially if it has custody or visitation provisions. A protections order is one tool that can help you gain your independence and stop your abuser from hurting you and your children. You should contact a domestic violence advocate and qualified attorney in your area to discuss the best ways to ensure the safety of you and your children.

You can always get more information from the National Coalition Against Domestic Violence at www.ncadv.org or call the hotline: 1-800-799-SAFE. Many communities offer shelters for battered women and children. Details on these shelters are available from police, crisis intervention services, hospitals, churches, family courts, departments of health and human services, or women's organizations such as the National Organization for Women.

Depending on your income, you may qualify for free or reduced legal services. Check with your local domestic violence shelter or bar association under the yellow pages or go to:

www.abanet.org/legalservices/public.html.

two: physical self-defense

Are you too scared to fight back? Too oppressed? Then, at least protect yourself and give yourself some options. Here are some things you can do to protect your body if you are being physically attacked:

Do you have nail polish remover? How about craft adhesive spray? These are extreme eye irritants, especially the adhesive. Keep these in a spray bottle in an easy-to-get-to place, and if you are being physically attacked, try to grab one and spray your attacker in the eyes. Then, run. Get far away from the attacker, because they are going to be really mad when their eyes clear up.

To help keep you from being choked, press your chin to your chest if they are approaching you in a threatening way. If they do grab you by the throat, turn your body in a circle to break their grip. Use your arms to push down on their arms to loosen the pressure.

If you are being hit, keep your forearms up and facing out. Use the muscle part of your forearms to protect your face and upper chest. Keep your elbows in as close to your body as possible.

You cannot withstand continuous blows to your face or temples, so think about the way a boxer moves and keep your hands up and try to cover your temples with your own fists, one on either side. Hardcover books can be held against your chest to protect you, but they can also be used against you, so be careful.

If you get hit in the face, really play possum. Act like you're knocked out. Practice this before it actually happens. Make sure you're in a fetal position, because the abuser will hit you a few more times to make sure you're not faking it.

If you are being pulled down by your hair, don't just fall backward. Go with the energy, turn into the attacker, and then run underneath the abuser's arm, close to their body, and run away from them. This will cause them to lose their grip on your hair, and you will be behind them with an opportunity to get away.

If you're getting slammed against the wall or floor, as you hit the surface, say, "Ugh," and tighten your stomach. This will help keep the blows from causing as much damage.

If you're lifted up off of the ground and held up to the wall by your neck or shoulders, kick the attacker in the shins as hard as you can. Keep your chin in and push down on his arms to push your body up and away, keeping your airway open as long as possible.

If you get thrown down on your back, try as best you can to keep your chin in and your elbows close to your chest over your breasts, and once again, try to guard your face with your hands. You will still get hit, but better on your hands than your face.

Get in the fetal position as much as possible, and most importantly, make the decision to get away from this person! This is not the kind of advice I like to give out. I want you to leave the situation rather than tolerate it, but in the meantime, these few tips should help keep you safer from permanent physical damage. Of course, you must realize that the longer you experience this abuse, the greater the emotional damage that is being done to you and your children.

three: mental self-defense

Do your best to try to diffuse arguments as much as possible while you are cooking dinner. There are so many things in the kitchen that can be used to hurt you. Of course, you could use those same things to protect yourself if you can get up the nerve.

How can you diffuse a bomb? It's not easy. You must become an expert. Abusers are like bombs. If you can figure out the triggers, maybe you can diffuse more explosions and beatings until you can get out. Maybe when he gets home, he is just in a bad mood because he worked all day, and he thinks you haven't been doing anything. Thank him for working so hard and show him some things that you did for him today so he wouldn't have to worry when he got home.

Or you can try this: If he pushes you, say something like, "Wow, you are really getting strong and in shape. I can tell." Sounds silly and stupid, but it can work. The key is identifying the triggers that make him go off. Is it anything in particular? Beer? Kids screaming? Money talk? Think about the triggers and use your words to diffuse the bomb. Is there something he absolutely loves or a subject that he just really likes talking about? Sometimes bringing up favorite topics will diffuse the situation. If he is a garbage truck driver and hates his job, have you ever asked him about how all that big machinery works? Compliment his ability to do the job, perhaps by saying, "It looks really complicated to operate that truck. I don't think I could ever learn how to run such an expensive piece of equipment. I am very proud of you."

Do you see what I mean by trying to stop the trigger from being pulled. Use what you have to try to keep the bomb from going off. In the meantime, follow my plan to get away, get your steps ready and get the legal help that you need.

Let me ask you a few questions. Did you almost die this time? Or was the beating not as bad this time? How much more are you going to take? How much more can your body take? Your kids? Your family? You must understand that it's not going to get any better.

Mentally, you may think you're worthless. Well, you're not! You're a kind human being, and you're too nice to be with someone who is treating you this way, and you deserve better. Your abuser has most likely brainwashed you into thinking that no one else will ever have you! Well, that's just not true. It's never true. Are you saying, "Poor me. I can't make it on my own?" Well, yes, yes, yes you can! There are angels all around you, people who will help you. They will. All you have to do is believe and ask! God's angels are all around us. I honestly believe that I have met many angels in my time right here on earth because God puts certain people in your life exactly when you need them. It's up to you to open your eyes and see them.

four: home self-defense

Once you've gotten the abuser out of the house or have gotten away to a new safe location, take some steps to fortify your home defenses.

1. Start having a female friend over (and maybe her kids if they're friends of your kids). It will help you feel better and safer. A lot of moms would love to get a break from their kids and/or husband once in a while and stay over.

2. If you can't afford a security system, make sure you have bushes (something thorny like a rose bush or pyracantha bush under each window. They are very pretty but can cause a major problem for someone who is trying to break in through a window). Go to your local hardware store and purchase stick-on contact alarms for your windows and your doors. They are inexpensive ($20-25 for a pack), easy to install, very effective, and very loud.

3. Secure all your windows and sliding glass doors with wooden broomsticks or dowels cut to the right length.

4. Keep plants, lamps, or furniture in front of windows or doors. This will deter someone from breaking in, because they know you will hear them.

5. Purchase a garden sprayer and fill it with nail polish remover and keep it by your bed. This is an extreme eye irritant, and if you find a stranger in your room at night, don't hesitate to use it; then run.

6. Keep a knife under your pillow.

7. Make sure there is something you can reach in every room to use for protection to put space between you and your attacker.

8. Keep your car keys on your nightstand, and use the remote (if you hear something) to set off your car alarm. You can also keep an extra contact alarm by your bed to create a loud alarm noise. Many intruders will assume that you have an alarm system that is automatically sending the police. Only you know that it's a stick-on alarm.

9. Let your neighbors know what's going on with your estranged attacker and ask them to be on the lookout for anyone or anything that looks suspicious around your house.

10. Change your cell number.

11. Important: If you have recently left an abusive partner and relocated, during this time, your kids should not have access to the phone—their phone or yours. This is not a typical separation if you've been in a

violent, abusive situation. However, the abuser is still their parent, and your kids probably still love them. It would be very easy for the abuser to charm his way into finding out where you are. Until things have calmed and you have a secure situation, you must be clear about this with your kids.

12. If you are in the home you had with your attacker, change all the locks and control all the keys.

fun and practical:
how shopping for shoes can save your life

Go to a secondhand store and buy a pair of men's used, size 14-16 work boots or buy an inexpensive pair at your local store. Acquire a pair of men's socks as well. Take them home, get out some paint of different colors, and splatter it all over the boots. Put some mud and dirt on them too. If you want, tie them to the back of your car and drag them down the road a while! In other words, make them look like they are well used on a daily basis.

Take the socks and scrub them in some dirt to make them look worked in too. Now, strategically place them by the door you enter and exit. This in itself provides a measure of security for little or no cost, because there is really no way of telling whether you have a big bruiser of a boyfriend inside or not. This will sway potential attackers away from your home. It never hurts to throw a smashed, manly beer can or a crumpled cigarette box on them too. Make sure you routinely move these boots around and take them inside; then move them out again in case someone is periodically checking on or stalking your house.

a new philosophy

There are all kinds of self-help books out there. The first question you have to ask yourself is, "Do I want help?" Maybe you like suffering. Maybe suffering is the only thing you've ever known, which can certainly be the case, but that doesn't mean that you can't change it. Starting now. Take a look around. God has placed angels all around you every day. You just need to open your eyes! Fight Like A Girl! It's all in your attitude. Attitude is the key element to how everything in this world works. Think about it. Poor attitude equals poor work ethic. Good attitudes affect positive results.

I know what you are thinking. I have been there. You are saying to yourself, "I have tried being nice, but he still hits me. I have tried to do everything

right and still no success. Even at work, I have done my job and have tried to please my boss and still, no promotion." Let me clear a few things up for you. See, the problem is that you have spent your whole life trying to please others and doing what you can to make them happy with you. The problem is that your whole life you have tried to be a pleaser. Guess what? That is your problem. First of all, you have to make yourself happy. Do your job with purpose because you can, not because you feel like you must. Do your job well because you like doing a good job.

Please your husband or boyfriend or mate because you care about them and not because this will happen or that will happen if you don't. Why would you want to please someone who continues to belittle you anyway? Is that how you are repaid for your affection and work? Is that acceptable? You may live in a luxurious house and drive a Mercedes, but is it worth it if you pay for it by letting him beat on you or humiliate you? Are you serving someone so that you can be abused? Wake up! Or maybe you just want to keep the family together? What kind of a message are you passing on to your children! What philosophies are you ingraining in their psyches? Needless to say, if they are raised in an abusive environment, they will probably be abusers themselves. Children learn by example. What is "normal" to them is what they have experienced.

If you don't muster up the courage to make a major change, I hope you have a good job and financial planner. Why? Because if you stay in an abusive relationship, one of three things is (or all three are) going to affect your kids. One: you and your children have a good chance of being killed by your abuser. Two: you and your kids will definitely need therapy if you hope to be emotionally free from the abuse. Three: you and your kids will most likely experience some type of addiction. So all of this is going to cost you—if you're still around to pay. Maybe not today, but definitely in the future.

My point is: Get out now! It is your fault if you stay in an abusive relationship. It is your fault if your kids are screwed up for life. "No," you say. "It's my abuser's fault." No, it's not. Just like me. It was my fault that I stayed in a mentally, then physically abusive, relationship. Mine and mine alone.

Here's the main obstacle I see to getting out of abusive relationships: the mistaken belief that, "They won't do it again." That is just a subliminal message that means, "I am scared that I can't make it on my own." Guess what? It's okay…to be scared. The best moments of my life involved being scared to death just before the ultimate reward came. Breaking free. Risking everything. Practicing for forty hours a week for years just for a chance, for that one moment that lasts about one minute and thirty seconds. Petrified, but I was petrified with a plan. I planned. Being scared with a plan makes the difference. Having a plan is the difference between success and failure.

I was scared, but I made a plan and followed it through and got away from my abusive husband. I was scared, but I did win the World Karate Championships not just once but seven times. I was scared, but I did make it on my own and ultimately had much greater success than I ever would have staying in my fallen relationship because I was scared about going out on my own.

So, be scared. Plan to be scared in achieving your goals. But, Fight Like A Girl and be smarter. It's okay to cry and be happy at the same time. It's okay to let loose and be scared to death about what is going to happen when you risk everything. Make a plan. Take the leap. Stick to the plan as closely as possible, but

be willing to make adjustments for the brick walls, cement blocks, and birds in your path.

Let's define the obstacles. Brick walls: Your boss or your coworker who does everything in her power to make you look bad and take credit for what you do. Your attorney who hasn't gotten your restraining order done or your separation agreement completed. Not being able to find childcare. How are you going to start over with no childcare?

Cement blocks. (Here in the south, we call 'em cinder blocks): When you can't find a job. When you studied as hard as you could and still failed the exam. When you got your nails done, fixed your hair, and still didn't get the date.

Then the birds. Yes, the birds. Just when you least expect it, some seagull will fly over and dump on your head, in your hair, and on your windshield. Of course, you'll have no wiper fluid left. Seagulls! They're the worst for this. They swoop down and splat just when you least expect it—at the beach, on the sidewalk, or through your window traveling down the road. It gets in your hair, on your arm, running down the side of your face, into your mascara. Do you want to know what a bird is? It's when the engine in your car blows up, the refrig-

erator dies, the proposal you just spent weeks on is ready for presentation and you accidentally delete it when you spill coffee on your keypad. When the school calls, and your child has fallen and broken his arm in three places, and even though you have insurance, your deductible is so high you have to pay for most of it anyway.

You see where I am going with this. No wonder you're scared. I certainly was scared writing this book. I have never written a self-help book. I have always helped people in person, but I can't be everywhere, and I want to do more. So I learned as much as I could about how this works and took a look around and decided, "I can do this." You can make your plan work, too. Plan to be scared. The key is to plan the best you can with what you have, and if you don't have it, find someone who does.

There are angels. God works through people. Do you understand? I don't know what your beliefs are, but you obviously need help. I am telling you how to get where you want to be. There are people in your everyday life who can help you with almost anything. It's true! Anyone who has achieved any goal— whether it be someone trying to get out of an abusive relationship, a parent trying to raise their children,

an employee trying to achieve advancement at work, an entrepreneur opening a business, or a person just trying to find a place to live—has received help from someone. Ask and you shall receive. Now, you can't just ask one person for help that perhaps isn't able to at that time and say, "Well, I give up."

It's your perspective that has kept you from achieving what you want or getting what you need to survive. For example, you may say, "I don't have a trade because I have been a housewife and raising kids for the last ten years." Listen to what you do have. "I have over ten years of experience in children's clothing, education, and household management."

Many companies now allow mothers to work from home, and there are companies that provide on-site childcare. Don't just believe me? Click onto any working mother related website, and you will find companies that compete to keep women on the job. If you want to find a good job, it's not what you know; it's who you know. If you just moved out and to a new town and don't know anyone, if you're starting on your own with no job and no clue, find out where employees of good companies go to lunch. Have coffee there or a soda. You may be the little fish in the big pond, but if you shadow the big fish, you will find out where the food is. Strike up a conversation, even in the coffee line; start talking about your children or your pet. If you notice this person gets out of a great-looking car, strike up conversation about their car.

One thing I have found in marketing yourself in any situation is that if you find something a person mentions that brightens their eye (if they mention their dog, remember what kind; if they mention their child, remember their name), when you see them again, and you will, because most coffee and lunch people frequent the same places every day, say, "Oh, hello again. How is your daughter, Sadie?" or "How's your Dalmatian doing?" This breaks down barriers for further conversation, and the next thing you know they will be asking where are you from, where you live, where you work, etc. This opens the door for you to say that you just relocated and are looking for job opportunities in the area. There you go. This is just one example.

I am not saying you should do this every day, but I am saying that you can do this in addition to putting in applications, searching the paper and employment agencies, and using other traditional job-search methods. This conversational technique works well in trying to get where you want or need to be.

Surround yourself with people who are already where you want to be, and start formulating a plan. Like I said, there are angels all around you. Maybe your friend can't help in a given situation, but they know someone who knows someone.

Let's review. It's okay to be scared. Be scared with a plan. Everyone has something to offer and experiences they can use to make a living. Everyone. Shadow the big fish. Angels are all around you. Simple. Get smart. Get away. Get a job. Do it for yourself and for your kids. Achieve your goals.

There's your Fight Like a Girl survival plan!

you can do this

1. People

☐   Identify the people who are going to help you.

☐   • Nearest shelter

☐   • Family members

☐   • Others

☐   Plan A

☐   Plan B

2. Tell

☐ Tell your helpers exactly and specifically what you need them to do. Who, what, where, when, why, and how.

☐ Plan A

☐ Plan B

3. Plan

☐ Determine your getaway plan.

☐ Plan A

☐ Plan B

4. Lodging

☐ Determine two safe options for where to go as soon as you escape.

☐ • Shelter

☐ • Family

☐ • Friends

☐ • Other

☐ Plan A

☐ Plan B

5. Money

☐ You have enough cash hidden away to make it where you are going.

☐ Plan A

☐ Plan B

6. Transportation

☐ Determine two getaway vehicles/plans.

☐ Plan A

☐ Plan B

7. Contacts.

☐ All the players contact information is saved in your phone and written in several places. You have 911 on speed dial or favorites.

☐ Plan A

☐ Plan B

8. Gather

☐ • Mace, pepper spray, stun gun

☐ • Driver's license

☐ • Passport

☐ • Birth certificate (you and kids)

☐ • Kids photo IDs (if you have)

☐ • Kids school records

☐ • If using a car: registration, insurance, and title (if available)

☐ • Clothes, toiletries, shoes
(you and kids)

☐ • Kids' comfort items (teddy
bears, blanket, favorite
book, crayons)

☐ • A pay-as-you-go cell phone
with new number

☐ • Your and kids' medical records

☐ • Ways to get them out
of the house

☐ Plan A

☐ Plan B

9. Leaving day and time

☐ Plan A

☐ Plan B

10. Excuses and alternates—

☐ If you are caught leaving by your partner or if one of your helpers misses a cue and you have to deviate from the initial plan.

☐ Plan A

☐ Plan B

11. Ideas to get on your feet financially

☐ Give this some thought and have a list of opportunities to check into once you're safe.

☐ Plan A

☐ Plan B

end notes

Chapter One:

1. U.S. Department of Justice, "National Crime Victimization Survey" (Washington, DC: 2003.)

2. U.S. Department of Justice, "Prevalence, Incidence, and Consequences of Violence Against Women" (Washington DC: November 1998.)

3. Tjaden, Patricia & Thoennes, Nancy. National Institute of Justice and the Centers of Disease Control, "Prevention, Extent, Nature and Consequences of Intimate Partner Violence: Findings from the National Violence Against Women Survey" (Washington, DC: 2000.)

4. Federal Bureau of Investigation, "Uniform Crime Reports: Crime in the United States 2000" (Washington DC: 2001.)

5. U.S. Department of Justice, "Bureau of Justice Statistics: Intimate Partner Violence in the United States" (Washington, DC: December 2006.)

6. Centers for Disease Control and Prevention, "National Centers for Injury Prevention and Control: Costs of Intimate Partner Violence Against Women in the United States" (Atlanta, Georgia: 2003.)

7. Ibid.

8. L.E. Ohlin & M. H. Tonry, "Family Violence" (Chicago, IL: University of Chicago Press, 1989). http://www.advocatesafehouse.org/index.php?option=com_content&view=article&id=50&Itemid=58

9. http://www.rainn.org/get-information/statistics/sexual-assault-victims (1998)

10. http://www.rainn.org/get-information/statistics/sexual-assault-victims/ (2003)

11. http://www.rainn.org/get-information/statistics/sexual-assault-offenders/ (1997)

12. http://www.uvavictimsofrape.com/about.htm (2009)

13. According to the U.S. Department of Justice's, " National Crime Victimization Survey," (Washington D.C.: 1997)

Chapter Three:

1. U.S. Department of Justice, "National Crime Victimization Survey." (Washington, DC: 2003.)

2. Samuel C. McQuade III, Ph.D. and Neel Sampat, Study of Internet and At-risk Behaviors. Rochester Institute of Technology Center for Multidisciplinary Studeis, June 18, 2008.

3. Baltimore Crime Examiner Arlene Karridis related links   http://www.missingkids.com/missingkids/servlet/PublicHomeServlet?LanguageCountry=en_US

http://www.childconnection.org/missing.html

http://www.pollyklaas.org/about/

4. U.S. Department of Justice, "Child Exploitation and Obscenity Section." (Washington D.C: Accessed October 31, 2007)

5. http://www.ncjrs.gov/html/ojjdp/nismart (2004)

6. Harris Interactive, "McAfee Study" http://www.mcafee.com/us/about/press/corporate/2008/20081022_095000_x.html (October 2008.)

7. Wolak, Janis, et al. "Unwanted and Wanted Exposure to Online Pornography in a National Sample of Youth Internet Users." Pediatrics 119 (2007); 247-257.

8. Ibid.

9. Bryan-Low, Cassel and Pringle, David. "Sex Cells: Wireless Operators Find That Racy Cellphone Video Drives Surge in Broadband Use." The Wall Street Journal. (May 12, 2005.)

10. IDC technology research firm as quoted on http://erlc.com/issues/quick-facts/por/ (2004.)

11. Juniper Research, "Adult to Mobile: Personal Services – Fourth Edition" http://www.juniperresearch.com/shop/viewreport.php?id=96 (November 2007.)

12. National Center for Missing & Exploited Children, Crimes Against Children Research Center, Office of Juvenile Justice and Delinquency Prevention. "Online Victimization of Youth: Five Years Later"

(Washington DC: December 4, 2006.) http://www. unh.edu/ccrc/pdf/CV138.pdf.

13. Rideout, Victoria, Tobert, Donald and Foehr, Ulla. "Generation M: Media in the Lives of 8-18 Year-Olds," The Henry J. Kaiser Family Foundation. (Washington DC: November 17, 2006.)

14. Ibid.

15. Ibid.

16. Ibid.

17. Ibid.

18. Ibid.

19. U.S. Department of Justice, "National Crime Victimization Survey." (Washington, DC: 2003.)

20. Security on Campus, Inc. www.securityoncampus. org

21. US Department of Justice. Office of Community Oriented Policing Services. No. 17 (Washington D.C. 2002)

22. National Center for Victims of Crime, "Stalking Facts" http://www.ncvc.org/src/main. aspx?dbID=DB_statistics195

23. Ibid.

Chapter Four

1. U.S. Bureau of Justice Statistics, "Criminal victimization in the United States Statistical Tables" (Washington D.C 3/2/2010 NCJ 227669)

2. The National Center for Missing and Exploited Children,

   http://www.ncmec.org/missingkids

3. Domestic Violence Resource Center, http://www.dvrc-or.org/domestic/violence/resources/C61/

4. Ibid

5. A Joint Research Project, Maine Department of Labor and Family Crisis Services, Kim Ridley, Johnn Rioux, Kim C. Lim Ph.D., Desirae Mason, Kate Faragher, Faye Luppi, J.D., Tracey Melody "Domestic Violence Survivors at Work: How Perpetrators Impact Employment" (Maine 2005)

6. Martin S. fiebert, Department of {Psychology, California Sate University, "Referenceing Examining Assaults by Women on Their Spouses or Male Partners," (California 2009)

7. C.Rennison. U.S. Dept. of Justice/Office, "Intimate partner violence" (Washington D.C. 2003) NXJ 19. 7838.

8. http://www.aardvarc.org/dv/statistics.shtml

9. Ibid.

10. Allstate Foundation National Poll on Domestic Violence, 2006. Lieberman Research Inc., "Tracking Survey conducted for The Advertising Council and the Family Violence Prevention Fund,"(July – October 1996)

11. http://www.grabstats.com/statcategorymain

12. U.S. Department of Justice, "National Crime Victimization Survey." (Washington, DC: 2003.)